Tasty Bean Recipes for Daily Meals

Jacques P. Markham

All rights reserved.

Copyright © 2024 Jacques P. Markham

Tasty Bean Recipes for Daily Meals : Delicious Legume Dishes to Elevate Your Everyday Cooking Game

Funny helpful tips:

Maintain transparency in financial dealings; it builds trust with stakeholders.

Rotate reading based on mood and need; sometimes you need motivation, other times relaxation or knowledge.

Introduction

In a world where the humble bean has long been overshadowed by flashier food trends, it's time to shine a spotlight on this versatile and nutritious powerhouse. This book is not just a collection of recipes; it's a celebration of beans in all their glory, from the hearty warmth of a slow-cooked chili to the zesty freshness of a black bean and corn salad. This book is an ode to beans' incredible versatility, showcasing them in a dazzling array of dishes that will change the way you think about these humble legumes.

At the heart of this cookbook lies a simple truth: beans are for everyone. Whether you're a seasoned chef or a kitchen novice, a meat-lover or a vegetarian, there's something in these pages for you. From the comfort of Chicken and Chickpea Rice Pilaf to the innovative twist of Garbanzo Bean Chocolate Cake (Gluten-Free!), each recipe is a testament to the bean's ability to seamlessly adapt to different flavors, cuisines, and meal types.

Imagine starting your day with a hearty Roasted Sweet Potato, Black Bean, and Chorizo Breakfast Bowl, or unwinding in the evening with a comforting bowl of Red Lentil Soup with Lemon-Mint Yogurt. Picture yourself impressing guests with the elegance of Chickpea Maltagliati e Fagioli or enjoying a quiet, nourishing meal with the Simple Turkey Chili. "Beans and Legumes Cookbook" takes you on a global culinary journey, from the zesty streets of Mexico with its Black Beans and Rice to the aromatic kitchens of India with Kale and Chickpeas, without ever leaving the comfort of your home.

Moreover, this cookbook is a celebration of healthful eating. Beans and legumes are not only rich in proteins but are also great sources of fiber, vitamins, and minerals, contributing to a balanced diet in the most delicious way possible. Whether you're looking to incorporate more plant-based proteins into your meals, manage your budget better, or simply add variety to your cooking repertoire, beans offer a world of possibilities.

For those concerned about time and convenience, fear not. This book includes recipes that span from the slow-simmered richness of Boston Baked Beans to the instant gratification of Quick Black Beans and Rice. The Instant Pot Baked Beans and Slow Cooker Chicken Taco Soup stand testament to the fact that in the world of beans, there's a perfect balance between slow-cooked flavor and modern-day efficiency.

And let's not forget about the sweets. Beans in desserts? Absolutely. The Black Bean Brownies and the Garbanzo Bean Chocolate Cake will challenge your perceptions and delight your taste buds, proving once and for all that beans can comfortably occupy any course of the meal.

This book is more than just a collection of recipes; it's a toolkit for creativity, a gateway to more sustainable eating, and a treasure trove of flavors waiting to be discovered. Whether you're looking to spice up your meal plans, find new family favorites, or simply explore the vast culinary potential of beans and legumes, this book is your companion on a journey that promises to be as enriching as it is delicious.

Welcome to the bean revolution. It's time to rediscover these culinary gems and give them the place they deserve in our kitchens and on our plates.

Contents

CHICKEN AND CHICKPEA RICE PILAF 1
MEXICAN BLACK BEANS AND RICE 3
INSTANT POT BAKED BEANS 4
LENTILS WITH GROUND BEEF AND RICE 6
ROASTED SWEET POTATO, BLACK BEAN, AND CHORIZO BREAKFAST BOWLS ... 8
INDIAN KALE WITH CHICKPEAS 10
RED LENTIL SOUP WITH LEMON-MINT YOGURT 11
CHICKPEA MALTAGLIATI E FAGIOLI 13
SLOW COOKER CHICKEN TACO SOUP 15
QUINOA AND BLACK BEANS 17
HOMEMADE BLACK BEAN VEGGIE BURGERS 18
DEBDOOZIE'S BLUE RIBBON CHILI 20
ITALIAN SAUSAGE SOUP 22
IT'S CHILI BY GEORGE!! 23
ADDICTIVE SWEET POTATO BURRITOS 25
MEXICAN BEAN SALAD 26
REFRIED BEANS WITHOUT THE REFRY 28
CHA CHA'S WHITE CHICKEN CHILI 29
SLOW COOKER TACO SOUP 31
SIMPLE TURKEY CHILI 33
HUMMUS 34
DELICIOUS BLACK BEAN BURRITOS 35
SIX CAN CHICKEN TORTILLA SOUP 37
THE BEST VEGETARIAN CHILI IN THE WORLD 38
BLACK BEAN AND SALSA SOUP 40
BLACK BEAN AND CORN QUESADILLAS 41
BLACK BEAN AND CORN SALAD 42
CHILI 44
LAURA'S QUICK SLOW COOKER TURKEY CHILI 46
SOUTHWESTERN EGG ROLLS 48

SPICY BEAN SALSA	50
SEAN'S FALAFEL AND CUCUMBER SAUCE	51
ZESTY QUINOA SALAD	53
BLACK BEAN AND COUSCOUS SALAD	55
RED LENTIL CURRY	56
SPICY BLACK BEAN VEGETABLE SOUP	58
BOSTON BAKED BEANS	60
WHITE BEAN CHICKEN CHILI	62
AUTHENTIC LOUISIANA RED BEANS AND RICE	64
WHITE CHILI WITH GROUND TURKEY	65
BLACK BEANS AND RICE	67
SWEET POTATO, CARROT, APPLE, AND RED LENTIL SOUP	69
BASIC HAM AND BEAN SOUP	71
CREAMY WHITE CHILI	73
QUINOA BLACK BEAN BURGERS	74
MEXICAN CASSEROLE	76
FANTASTIC BLACK BEAN CHILI	77
BEAKER'S VEGETABLE BARLEY SOUP	80
SLOW COOKER CHILI	81
GRANDMA'S SLOW COOKER VEGETARIAN CHILI	84
VEGAN BLACK BEAN SOUP	86
GARBANZO BEAN CHOCOLATE CAKE (GLUTEN FREE!)	87
BLACK BEAN BROWNIES	88
SEVEN LAYER TORTILLA PIE	90
PAT'S BAKED BEANS	91
SLOW COOKER LENTIL AND HAM SOUP	94
LAYERED CHICKEN AND BLACK BEAN ENCHILADA CASSEROLE	95
BEST BLACK BEANS	97
LENTIL SOUP WITH LEMON	98
ANDREA'S PASTA FAGIOLI	100
LENTILS AND RICE WITH FRIED ONIONS (MUJADARRAH)	101
SLOW COOKER SPICY BLACK-EYED PEAS	102
CHICKEN AND CORN CHILI	104

SMOKIN' SCOVILLES TURKEY CHILI	105
SPICED SWEET ROASTED REDPEPPER HUMMUS	107
JUST LIKE WENDY'S® CHILI	109
CHICKEN FIESTA SALAD	111
CORN AND BLACK BEAN SALAD	113
MOCK TUNA SALAD	114
MAKE AHEAD LUNCH WRAPS	115
EXTRA EASY HUMMUS	116
VEGETARIAN KALE SOUP	117
LENTIL AND SAUSAGE SOUP	119
BLACK BEANS AND PORK CHOPS	120
TEX-MEX TURKEY SOUP	121
ITALIAN VEGETABLE SOUP	123
GREEK PASTA WITH TOMATOES ANDWHITE BEANS	126
WHITE CHILI I	127
GREEK GARBANZO BEAN SALAD	129
MIDDLE EASTERN RICE WITH BLACKBEANS AND CHICKPEAS	130
MOROCCAN LENTIL SOUP	132
EASY RED BEANS AND RICE	133
BLACK-EYED PEA GUMBO	135
VEGETARIAN MEXICAN INSPIREDSTUFFED PEPPERS	136
PASTA FAGIOLI	139
BROWN RICE AND BLACK BEANCASSEROLE	140
JERRE'S BLACK BEAN AND PORK TENDERLOIN SLOW COOKER CHILI	142
ROASTED CHICKPEAS	143
AWARD WINNING CHILI	144
EASY WHITE CHILI	146
BRAZILIAN BLACK BEAN STEW	147
"PANTRY RAID" CHICKENENCHILADA CASSEROLE	149
HAM BONE SOUP	151
WHITE CHILI	152
PUMPKIN BLACK BEAN SOUP	153
BLACK BEAN SALAD	154

SPINACH AND LEEK WHITE BEANSOUP 156
THE ULTIMATE CHILI 157
HEATHER'S CILANTRO, BLACKBEAN, AND CORN SALSA 159
BUTTER BEAN BURGERS 160
QUINOA AND BLACK BEAN CHILI 161
HAM AND BEANS 163
VEGAN SPLIT PEA SOUP 164
NAVY BEAN SOUP 166
LENTILS AND SPINACH 167
SWEET POTATO AND BLACK BEANCHILI 169
BEAN QUESADILLAS 171
TERRY'S TEXAS PINTO BEANS 174
ESPINACAS CON GARBANZOS (SPINACH WITH GARBANZO BEANS) 175
PASTA E FAGIOLI A LA CHEZ IVANO 176
VEGAN BEAN TACO FILLING 178
ONE SKILLET MEXICAN QUINOA 179
VEGAN RED LENTIL SOUP 180
VEGETARIAN MOUSSAKA 182
PORK CHALUPAS 185
MEXICAN QUESADILLA CASSEROLE 186
EASY CHICKEN FAJITA SOUP 188
CREAMY ITALIAN WHITE BEAN SOUP 190
CALICO BEAN CASSEROLE 192
PUMPKIN CHILI 194
CROCK-POT CHICKEN CHILI 195
TEXAS CAVIAR 196
MEATIEST VEGETARIAN CHILI FROMYOUR SLOW COOKER 199
WASHABINAROS CHILI 200
EASY HOMEMADE CHILI 203
CHILI RICK'S 204
SPICED QUINOA 205
BEST BEEF ENCHILADAS 207
SPINACH LENTIL SOUP 209

BLACK BEAN CHILI	210
SPICY BLACK BEAN CAKES	212
EASY HUMMUS	214
MINESTRONE SOUP	215
SWISS CHARD WITH GARBANZO BEANS AND FRESH TOMATOES	217
UNSLOPPY JOES	218
MEXICAN PASTA	220
VEGGIE VEGETARIAN CHILI	221
LEBANESE-STYLE RED LENTIL SOUP	224
SLOW COOKER HOMEMADE BEANS	226
SUE'S TACO SALAD	227
CHICKPEA SALAD WITH RED ONION AND TOMATO	228
APRICOT LENTIL SOUP	229
MUSHROOM LENTIL BARLEY STEW	230
QUICK AND EASY REFRIED BEANS	232
CHILI CON CARNE	233
SLOW COOKER LENTILS AND SAUSAGE	235
MICHELLE'S BLONDE CHICKEN CHILI	236
QUICK BLACK BEANS AND RICE	239
JALAPENO HUMMUS	240
VEGETARIAN CHILI	241
APPLE BACON TOMATO SOUP	242
LENTIL SOUP	244
TOMATO-CURRY LENTIL STEW	245
TASTY LENTIL TACOS	246
CHICKEN AND LENTILS	247
COWBOY CAVIAR	249
TACO SALAD	250
MEXICAN BEAN AND RICE SALAD	252
SMOKY CHIPOTLE HUMMUS	253
SOUTHERN HAM AND BROWN BEANS	255
PUB-STYLE VEGETARIAN CHILI	256
VEGETARIAN TORTILLA STEW	258

VEGETARIAN TORTILLA STEW	259
INDIAN DAHL WITH SPINACH	261
BEST BEAN SALAD	262
BAKED FALAFEL	264
ENCHILADA CASSEROLE	265

CHICKEN AND CHICKPEA RICE PILAF

Servings: 6 | Prep: 20m | Cooks: 1h9m | Total: 1h29m

NUTRITION FACTS

Calories: 343.2 | Carbohydrates: 37.4g | Protein: 24.9g | Cholesterol: 69mg | Sodium: 1376mg

INGREDIENTS

- 1 tablespoon butter
- 1 tablespoon vegetable oil
- 1 onion, diced
- 1 (15 ounce) can chickpeas, drained
- 1 cup long-grain brown rice
- 2 teaspoons salt, divided
- 2 teaspoons ground black pepper, divided
- 2 teaspoons ground cayenne pepper, divided
- 1 teaspoon dried thyme
- 2 cups chicken broth

- 6 eaches chicken drumsticks

DIRECTIONS

1. Preheat the oven to 425 degrees F (220 degrees C).
2. Melt butter with oil in a large saucepan over low heat. Add onion; cook and stir until translucent, 7 to 10 minutes. Add chickpeas and cook until heated through, 3 to 5 minutes. Add rice; cook and stir until translucent and coated in oil, 4 to 5 minutes. Remove from heat.
3. Season drumsticks with 1 teaspoon salt, 1 teaspoon black pepper, and 1 teaspoon cayenne pepper.
4. Heat a large cast iron skillet over medium-high heat. Cook drumsticks until skin is golden brown and crispy on all sides, about 10 minutes. Transfer to a plate.
5. Pour chicken broth into a deep saucepan and bring to a boil. Season with remaining salt, black pepper, and cayenne pepper; add thyme. Reduce heat to a simmer.
6. Transfer chickpea-rice mixture to an oven-proof cast iron skillet. Pour in the chicken broth and mix. Place drumsticks on top and cover skillet tightly with aluminum foil.
7. Bake in the preheated oven until rice is tender, 30 to 40 minutes. Remove aluminum foil, raise oven temperature to 450 degrees F (230 degrees C); continue baking until rice is crispy on top, 10 to 15 minutes more.

MEXICAN BLACK BEANS AND RICE

Servings: 4 | Prep: 10m | Cooks: 20m | Total: 30m

NUTRITION FACTS

Calories: 304 | Carbohydrates: 49.7g | Protein: 10.5g | Cholesterol: 0mg | Sodium: 668.8mg

INGREDIENTS

- 2 tablespoons coconut oil
- 1 teaspoon chili powder
- 1 teaspoon garlic powder
- 1 teaspoon ground cumin
- 1 teaspoon ground coriander
- 2 stalks celery, chopped
- 2 teaspoons chopped fresh oregano
- 2 teaspoons chopped fresh cilantro
- 1 (15 ounce) can black beans, rinsed and drained
- 1/2 cup mild salsa
- 1/4 cup water, or as needed
- 2 cups cooked white rice

- 1 tomato, chopped
- 1 pinch salt to taste
- 1/2 cup frozen corn

DIRECTIONS

1. Heat coconut oil in a large skillet over medium-low heat. Add chili powder, garlic powder, cumin, and coriander; fry until fragrant, about 30 seconds. Add celery, cook and stir until softened, 3 to 5 minutes.
2. Add tomato, frozen corn, oregano, and cilantro; stir to coat. Stir in black beans and salsa. Bring to a simmer and cook for 10 to 15 minutes, adding water as needed to keep the mixture saucy.
3. Remove from the heat and stir in cooked rice until coated. Season with salt.

INSTANT POT BAKED BEANS

Servings: 12 | Prep: 15m | Cooks: 1h15m | Total: 2h10m | Additional: 40m

NUTRITION FACTS

Calories: 320.6 | Carbohydrates: 36.2g | Protein: 11.1g | Cholesterol: 17.3mg | Sodium: 392.4mg

INGREDIENTS

- 8 cups water

- 1 pound dry navy beans, rinsed and picked through

- 1 tablespoon olive oil

- 6 ounces salt pork, diced

- 6 ounces bacon, cut into small pieces

- 1 small onion, minced

- 1 1/2 cups water, divided

- 1/4 cup ketchup

- 1/3 cup molasses

- 1/4 cup brown sugar

- 1 tablespoon yellow mustard

DIRECTIONS

1. Combine water and beans in a multi-functional pressure cooker (such as an Instant Pot®). Close and lock the lid. Select high pressure according to manufacturer's instructions; set timer for 15 minutes. Allow 10 to 15 minutes for pressure to build.
2. Release pressure using the natural-release method for 20 minutes; quick-release remaining pressure according to manufacturer's directions. Unlock and remove the lid. Drain

and rinse the beans with cold water and set aside. Rinse and wipe out Instant Pot® insert and place back into the pressure cooker.
3. Turn on Instant Pot® and select Saute function. Heat olive oil until shimmering, 2 to 3 minutes. Add salt pork, bacon, and onion and briefly cook until fat begins to render, 1 to 2 minutes. Pour in 1/2 cup water and scrape any brown bits off the bottom. Turn Instant Pot® off.
4. Whisk together ketchup, molasses, brown sugar, mustard, and remaining 1 cup water in a small bowl. Return cooked beans to the pot along with the ketchup mixture. Gently stir to combine. Close and lock the lid. Select high pressure according to manufacturer's instructions; set timer for 35 minutes. Allow 10 to 15 minutes for pressure to build.
5. Release pressure using the natural-release method for 20 minutes; quick-release any remaining pressure according to manufacturer's directions. Unlock and remove the lid. Beans will thicken upon cooling. Serve immediately or freeze portions for later.

LENTILS WITH GROUND BEEF AND RICE

Servings: 5 | Prep: 15m | Cooks: 40m | Total: 4h55m | Additional: 4h

NUTRITION FACTS

Calories: 473.5 | Carbohydrates: 41.5g | Protein: 27.8g | Cholesterol: 54.8mg | Sodium: 267.6mg

INGREDIENTS

- 1 cup dry lentils
- 5 cups water
- 1 cube beef bouillon
- 1/2 cup uncooked white rice
- 3 tablespoons vegetable oil
- 1 medium onion, chopped
- 2 tablespoons chopped red bell pepper
- 2 cloves garlic, minced
- 2 1/2 teaspoons ground cumin
- 1 pinch salt and ground black pepper to taste
- 1 pound lean ground beef
- 1 1/2 teaspoons ground paprika

DIRECTIONS

1. Place lentils in a bowl and cover with cold water. Soak for at least 4 hours.
2. Drain lentils and put in a large pot with 5 cups water and bouillon cube; bring to a boil. Reduce heat to a simmer and cook for 15 minutes. Add rice and simmer until rice and lentils are tender, 15 to 20 minutes.

3. Meanwhile, heat oil in a skillet over medium heat. Add onion, bell pepper, garlic, cumin, salt, and pepper; saute until onion is golden brown and tender, 5 to 7 minutes. Add ground beef; cook and stir until browned and crumbly, 7 to 9 minutes. Add paprika and cook for 1 more minute.
4. Add meat mixture to lentils and rice. Simmer over low heat for 5 to 10 minutes.

ROASTED SWEET POTATO, BLACK BEAN, AND CHORIZO BREAKFAST BOWLS

Servings: 4 | Prep: 15m | Cooks: 30m | Total: 45m

NUTRITION FACTS

Calories: 856.1 | Carbohydrates: 58.4g | Protein: 34.8g | Cholesterol: 260.7mg | Sodium: 2071.5mg

INGREDIENTS

- 2 eaches sweet potatoes, peeled and cut into 1/2-inch cubes
- 1 tablespoon olive oil
- 1/2 teaspoon ground cumin
- 1/2 teaspoon salt
- 1/4 teaspoon garlic powder
- 1 pound fresh Mexican chorizo sausage, casing removed

- 1/2 teaspoon salt
- 1 (15.5 ounce) can black beans, undrained
- 1/2 teaspoon ground cumin
- 1 tablespoon butter, or as needed
- 4 eggs
- 2 eaches avocados - peeled, pitted, and sliced

DIRECTIONS

1. Preheat the oven to 400 degrees F (200 degrees C). Line a baking sheet with parchment paper.
2. Combine sweet potatoes, olive oil, cumin, and salt in a medium bowl. Spread evenly on the prepared baking sheet.
3. Roast in the preheated oven, stirring after 10 minutes, until browned and cooked, 18 to 20 minutes total.
4. Meanwhile, combine black beans, cumin, salt, and garlic powder in a small saucepan over medium-low heat. Heat until warmed through, 8 to 10 minutes. Keep warm.
5. Brown chorizo in a large skillet over medium-high heat, breaking up any large clumps, for 5 to 6 minutes. Transfer chorizo to a paper towel-lined plate using a slotted spoon. Reserve about 1 tablespoon grease in the skillet, adding butter as needed to make up the difference.

6. Crack eggs into the skillet and cook until whites are set and yolks reach the desired doneness, 3 to 5 minutes.
7. Divide sweet potatoes, drained black beans, chorizo, and avocados between 4 bowls. Top each bowl with an egg.

INDIAN KALE WITH CHICKPEAS

Servings: 4 | Prep: 10m | Cooks: 15m | Total: 25m

NUTRITION FACTS

Calories: 211.7 | Carbohydrates: 30.9g | Protein: 6.4g | Cholesterol: 0mg | Sodium: 385.8mg

INGREDIENTS

- 2 tablespoons olive oil, or as needed
- 1 onion, finely chopped
- 1 red chile pepper, seeded and sliced
- 1 (14 ounce) can chickpeas, drained
- 1 tablespoon ground cumin
- 1/2 teaspoon ground turmeric
- 1 pinch ground cinnamon
- 1 pinch sea salt
- 1 lemon, zested and juiced
- 1 cup roughly chopped kale, or more to taste

- 1 teaspoon ground coriander

DIRECTIONS

1. Heat oil in a large frying pan or wok over medium-high heat. Add onion and chile pepper; saute until onion is tender, 5 to 7 minutes. Add chickpeas, cumin, coriander, turmeric, cinnamon, and salt; saute for 5 minutes. Pour in a splash of water, followed by lemon zest and juice. Season further to taste if desired.
2. Fold kale into the mixture until just wilted, 3 to 5 minutes. Remove from heat and serve.

RED LENTIL SOUP WITH LEMON-MINT YOGURT

Servings: 4 | Prep: 15m | Cooks: 45m | Total: 1h

NUTRITION FACTS

Calories: 294 | Carbohydrates: 41.2g | Fat: 8.2g | Protein: 15.8g | Cholesterol: 22mg

INGREDIENTS

- 2 tablespoons butter
- 1 cup red lentils
- 1 large yellow onion, diced
- 1 rib celery, diced

- 1 teaspoon kosher salt, or more to taste
- 3 tablespoons tomato paste, or more to taste
- 4 cloves garlic, crushed
- 2 teaspoons ground cumin
- 1/8 teaspoon cayenne pepper
- 1 quart chicken broth
- 1 large carrot, diced
- 6 leaves fresh mint, thinly sliced
- 1 pinch salt
- 1/2 teaspoon lemon zest
- 1/2 lemon, juiced
- 3 tablespoons plain Greek yogurt, or more to taste

DIRECTIONS

1. Melt butter in a saucepan over medium-high heat. Add onion, salt, and tomato paste. Cook, stirring often, until the onion softens and the tomato paste turns a deep brick red or brown color, 5 to 7 minutes.

2. Add garlic, cumin, and cayenne; cook, stirring, for 2 more minutes. Stir in the broth and bring to a simmer. Reduce heat to medium-low and add the lentils, celery, and carrots.
3. Stir and bring to a simmer. Cook, stirring occasionally, until the lentils and vegetables are very tender, 30 to 40 minutes.
4. Meanwhile, grind the mint and salt into a paste using a mortar and pestle. Add lemon zest, lemon juice, and yogurt, and stir together until combined. Refrigerate until ready to serve
5. Taste the soup and adjust seasoning as needed. Serve as-is or use an immersion blender to puree about half of the soup to achieve a creamier texture. Serve hot with spoonfuls of the lemon-mint yogurt.

CHICKPEA MALTAGLIATI E FAGIOLI
Servings: 4 | Prep: 30m | Cooks: 40m | Total: 9h20m | Additional: 8h10m

NUTRITION FACTS

Calories: 406.6 | Carbohydrates: 56g | Protein: 18.3g | Cholesterol: 0mg | Sodium: 88.5mg

INGREDIENTS

- 1 cup dried cranberry beans
- 20 eaches fresh green beans, cut into 1-inch pieces
- 2 sprigs fresh sage
- 10 eaches cherry tomatoes, quartered

- 1 sprig fresh rosemary
- 1 bay leaf
- kitchen twine
- 4 ounces chickpea lasagna sheets
- 2 tablespoons olive oil
- 1/2 cup diced onion
- 1/2 cup diced carrots
- 1/2 cup diced red bell pepper

- 1 clove garlic, minced
- 1 bird's eye chile, minced
- 4 cups water
- 1 cube vegetable bouillon
- 1 pinch salt and ground black pepper to taste
- 2 cups boiling water
- 4 teaspoons extra-virgin olive oil

DIRECTIONS

1. Soak beans in water, 8 hours to overnight.

2. Drain beans and briefly rinse under cold water. Allow to drain.
3. Tie sage, rosemary, and bay leaf with kitchen twine. Set aside. Break lasagna sheets into uneven pieces that are relatively the same size.
4. Heat a stovetop pressure cooker over medium-high heat. Add 2 tablespoons oil, onion, carrots, and red bell pepper; stir until onion is translucent. Add drained beans, herb bundle, green beans, cherry tomatoes, garlic, and chile pepper. Stir to ensure beans are evenly distributed. Add 4 cups water and bouillon cube. Secure the lid and bring to pressure. Cook for 8 minutes from the first whistle.
5. Turn off heat and allow pressure to release naturally according to manufacturer's instructions. Remove cover and discard herb bundle. Season stew with salt and pepper. Bring to a boil. Add pasta pieces a few at a time, stirring constantly to avoid sticking.
6. Add boiling water a little at a time if the stew becomes too thick. Stir frequently until pasta is tender yet firm to the bite, about 8 minutes. Ladle into 4 bowls. Top each bowl with 1 teaspoon extra-virgin olive oil.

SLOW COOKER CHICKEN TACO SOUP

Servings: 8 | Prep: 15m | Cooks: 7h | Total: 7h15m

NUTRITION FACTS

Calories: 433.7 | Carbohydrates: 42.3g | Protein: 27.2g | Cholesterol: 67.8mg | Sodium: 1596.8mg

INGREDIENTS

- 1 onion, chopped
- 1 (16 ounce) can chili beans
- 1 (15 ounce) can black beans
- 1 (15 ounce) can whole kernel corn, drained
- 1 (8 ounce) can tomato sauce
- 1 (12 fluid ounce) can or bottle beer
- 2 (10 ounce) cans diced tomatoes with green chilies, undrained
- 1 (1.25 ounce) package taco seasoning
- 3 whole skinless, boneless chicken breasts
- 1 (8 ounce) package shredded Cheddar cheese
- 1 (8 ounce) container sour cream
- 1 cup crushed tortilla chips

DIRECTIONS

1. Place the onion, chili beans, black beans, corn, tomato sauce, beer, and diced tomatoes in a slow cooker. Add taco seasoning, and stir to blend. Lay chicken breasts on top of the mixture, pressing down slightly until just covered by the other ingredients. Set slow cooker for low heat, cover, and cook for 5 hours.
2. Remove chicken breasts from the soup, and allow to cool long enough to be handled. Stir the shredded chicken back into the soup, and continue cooking for 2 hours. Serve topped with shredded Cheddar cheese, a dollop of sour cream, and crushed tortilla chips, if desired.

QUINOA AND BLACK BEANS

Servings: 10 | Prep: 15m | Cooks: 35m | Total: 50m

NUTRITION FACTS

Calories: 153 | Carbohydrates: 27.8g | Fat: 1.7g | Protein: 7.7g | Cholesterol: 0mg | Sodium: 517mg

INGREDIENTS

- 1 teaspoon vegetable oil
- 1 onion, chopped
- 3 cloves garlic, chopped
- 1/4 teaspoon cayenne pepper
- salt and ground black pepper to taste
- 1 cup frozen corn kernels

- 3/4 cup quinoa
- 2 (15 ounce) cans black beans, rinsed and drained
- 1 1/2 cups vegetable broth
- 1/2 cup chopped fresh cilantro
- 1 teaspoon ground cumin
- 1/4 teaspoon cayenne pepper

DIRECTIONS

1. Heat oil in a saucepan over medium heat; cook and stir onion and garlic until lightly browned, about 10 minutes.
2. Mix quinoa into onion mixture and cover with vegetable broth; season with cumin, cayenne pepper, salt, and pepper. Bring the mixture to a boil. Cover, reduce heat, and simmer until quinoa is tender and broth is absorbed, about 20 minutes.
3. Stir frozen corn into the saucepan, and continue to simmer until heated through, about 5 minutes; mix in the black beans and cilantro.

HOMEMADE BLACK BEAN VEGGIE BURGERS
Servings: 4 | Prep: 15m | Cooks: 20m | Total: 35m

NUTRITION FACTS

Calories: 198 | Carbohydrates: 33.1g | Fat: 3g | Protein: 11.2g | Cholesterol: 47mg | Sodium: 607mg

INGREDIENTS

- 1 (16 ounce) can black beans, drained and rinsed
- 1/2 green bell pepper, cut into 2 inch pieces
- 1/2 onion, cut into wedges
- 3 cloves garlic, peeled
- 1 egg
- 1 tablespoon chili powder
- 1 tablespoon cumin
- 1 teaspoon Thai chili sauce or hot sauce
- 1/2 cup bread crumbs

DIRECTIONS

1. If grilling, preheat an outdoor grill for high heat, and lightly oil a sheet of aluminum foil. If baking, preheat oven to 375 degrees F (190 degrees C), and lightly oil a baking sheet.
2. In a medium bowl, mash black beans with a fork until thick and pasty.

3. In a food processor, finely chop bell pepper, onion, and garlic. Then stir into mashed beans.
4. In a small bowl, stir together egg, chili powder, cumin, and chili sauce.
5. Stir the egg mixture into the mashed beans. Mix in bread crumbs until the mixture is sticky and holds together. Divide mixture into four patties.
6. If grilling, place patties on foil, and grill about 8 minutes on each side. If baking, place patties on baking sheet, and bake about 10 minutes on each side.

DEBDOOZIE'S BLUE RIBBON CHILI
Servings: 8 | Prep: 10m | Cooks: 1h | Total: 1h10m

NUTRITION FACTS

Calories: 480.2 | Carbohydrates: 24.9g | Protein: 26.7g | Cholesterol: 96.5mg | Sodium: 1366.2mg

INGREDIENTS

2
- pounds ground beef
- 1 (8 ounce) jar salsa
- 1/2 onion, chopped
- 4 tablespoons chili seasoning mix
- 1 teaspoon ground black pepper
- 1 (15 ounce) can light red kidney beans

- 1/2 teaspoon garlic salt
- 1 (15 ounce) can dark red kidney beans
- 2 1/2 cups tomato sauce

DIRECTIONS

1. In a large saucepan over medium heat, combine the ground beef and the onion and saute for 10 minutes, or until meat is browned and onion is tender. Drain grease, if desired.
2. Add the ground black pepper, garlic salt, tomato sauce, salsa, chili seasoning mix and kidney beans. Mix well, reduce heat to low and simmer for at least an hour.

ITALIAN SAUSAGE SOUP

Servings: 6 | Prep: 10m | Cooks: 40m | Total: 50m

NUTRITION FACTS

Calories: 385 | Carbohydrates: 22.5g | Fat: 24.4g | Protein: 18.8g | Cholesterol: 58mg | Sodium: 1259mg

INGREDIENTS

- 1 pound Italian sausage
- 1 clove garlic, minced
- 2 (14 ounce) cans beef broth
- 1 (14.5 ounce) can Italian-style stewed tomatoes
- 1 cup sliced carrots
- 1 (14.5 ounce) can great Northern beans, undrained
- 2 small zucchini, cubed
- 2 cups spinach - packed, rinsed and torn
- 1/4 teaspoon ground black pepper
- 1/4 teaspoon salt

DIRECTIONS

1. In a stockpot or Dutch oven, brown sausage with garlic. Stir in broth, tomatoes and carrots, and season with salt and pepper. Reduce heat, cover, and simmer 15 minutes.
2. Stir in beans with liquid and zucchini. Cover, and simmer another 15 minutes, or until zucchini is tender.
3. Remove from heat, and add spinach. Replace lid allowing the heat from the soup to cook the spinach leaves. Soup is ready to serve after 5 minutes.

IT'S CHILI BY GEORGE!!

Servings: 10 | Prep: 10m | Cooks: 1h45m | Total: 1h55m

NUTRITION FACTS

Calories: 305 | Carbohydrates: 25.5g | Fat: 13.7g | Protein: 22.3g | Cholesterol: 55mg

INGREDIENTS

- 2 pounds lean ground beef
- 1 (46 fluid ounce) can tomato juice
- 1 (29 ounce) can tomato sauce
- 1/8 teaspoon ground cayenne pepper
- 1/2 teaspoon white sugar
- 1/2 teaspoon dried oregano

- 1 (15 ounce) can kidney beans, drained and rinsed

- 1 (15 ounce) can pinto beans, drained and rinsed

- 1 1/2 cups chopped onion

- 1/4 cup chopped green bell pepper

- 1/2 teaspoon ground black pepper

- 1 teaspoon salt

- 1 1/2 teaspoons ground cumin

DIRECTIONS

1. Place ground beef in a large, deep skillet. Cook over medium-high heat until evenly brown. Drain, and crumble.
2. In a large pot over high heat combine the ground beef, tomato juice, tomato sauce, kidney beans, pinto beans, onions, bell pepper, cayenne pepper, sugar, oregano, ground black pepper, salt, cumin and chili powder. Bring to a boil, then reduce heat to low. Simmer for 1 1/2 hours. (Note: If using a slow cooker, set on low, add ingredients, and cook for 8 to 10 hours.)

ADDICTIVE SWEET POTATO BURRITOS

Servings: 6 | Prep: 15m | Cooks: 25m | Total: 40m

NUTRITION FACTS

Calories: 504.6 | Carbohydrates: 76.6g | Protein: 20g | Cholesterol: 19.8mg | Sodium: 1028.5mg

INGREDIENTS

- 1 tablespoon vegetable oil
- 1 onion, chopped
- 4 cloves garlic, minced
- 6 cups canned kidney beans, drained
- 2 cups water
- 2 teaspoons ground cumin
- 1 pinch cayenne pepper, or to taste
- 3 tablespoons soy sauce
- 4 cups mashed cooked sweet potatoes
- 12 (10 inch) flour tortillas, warmed

- 3 tablespoons chili powder
- 8 ounces shredded Cheddar cheese
- 4 teaspoons prepared mustard

DIRECTIONS

1. Preheat oven to 350 degrees F (175 degrees C).
2. Heat oil in a medium skillet and saute onion and garlic until soft. Mash beans into the onion mixture. Gradually stir in water; heat until warm, 2 to 3 minutes. Remove from heat and stir in the soy sauce, chili powder, mustard, cumin, and cayenne pepper.
3. Divide bean mixture and mashed sweet potatoes evenly between the tortillas; top with cheese. Fold tortillas burrito-style around the fillings and place on a baking sheet.
4. Bake in the preheated oven until warmed through, about 12 minutes.

MEXICAN BEAN SALAD

Servings: 8 | Prep: 15m | Cooks: 1h | Total: 1h15m | Additional: 1h

NUTRITION FACTS

Calories: 334 | Carbohydrates: 41.7g | Fat: 14.8g | Protein: 11.2g | Cholesterol: 0mg | Sodium: 1159mg

INGREDIENTS

- 1 (15 ounce) can black beans, rinsed and drained
- 1 (15 ounce) can kidney beans, drained
- 1 (15 ounce) can cannellini beans, drained and rinsed
- 1 green bell pepper, chopped
- 1 red bell pepper, chopped
- 1 (10 ounce) package frozen corn kernels
- 1 red onion, chopped
- 1/2 cup olive oil
- 1 tablespoon lemon juice
- 2 tablespoons white sugar
- 1 tablespoon salt
- 1 clove crushed garlic
- 1/4 cup chopped fresh cilantro
- 1/2 tablespoon ground cumin
- 1/2 tablespoon ground black pepper
- 1 dash hot pepper sauce

- 1/2 cup red wine vinegar
- 1/2 teaspoon chili powder
- 2 tablespoons fresh lime juice

DIRECTIONS

1. In a large bowl, combine beans, bell peppers, frozen corn, and red onion.
2. In a small bowl, whisk together olive oil, red wine vinegar, lime juice, lemon juice, sugar, salt, garlic, cilantro, cumin, and black pepper. Season to taste with hot sauce and chili powder.
3. Pour olive oil dressing over vegetables; mix well. Chill thoroughly, and serve cold.

REFRIED BEANS WITHOUT THE REFRY

Servings: 15 | Prep: 15m | Cooks: 8h | Total: 8h15m

NUTRITION FACTS

Calories: 139 | Carbohydrates: 25.4g | Fat: 0.5g | Protein: 8.5g | Cholesterol: 0mg | Sodium: 785mg

INGREDIENTS

- 1 onion, peeled and halved
- 3 cups dry pinto beans, rinsed
- 1/2 fresh jalapeno pepper, seeded and chopped
- 2 tablespoons minced garlic
- 1 3/4 teaspoons fresh ground black pepper
- 1/8 teaspoon ground cumin, optional
- 9 cups water
- 5 teaspoons salt

DIRECTIONS

1. Place the onion, rinsed beans, jalapeno, garlic, salt, pepper, and cumin into a slow cooker. Pour in the water and stir to combine. Cook on High for 8 hours, adding more water as needed. Note: if more than 1 cup of water has evaporated during cooking, then the temperature is too high.
2. Once the beans have cooked, strain them, and reserve the liquid. Mash the beans with a potato masher, adding the reserved water as needed to attain desired consistency.

CHA CHA'S WHITE CHICKEN CHILI
Servings: 4 | Prep: 10m | Cooks: 20m | Total: 30m
NUTRITION FACTS

Calories: 684 | Carbohydrates: 74.9g | Protein: 59.1g | Cholesterol: 101.9mg | Sodium: 1896mg

INGREDIENTS

- 1 tablespoon vegetable oil

- 1 onion, chopped

- 3 cloves garlic, crushed

- 1 (4 ounce) can diced jalapeno peppers

- 1 (4 ounce) can chopped green chile peppers

- 2 teaspoons ground cumin

- 1 teaspoon dried oregano

- 1 teaspoon ground cayenne pepper

- 2 (14.5 ounce) cans chicken broth

- 3 cups chopped cooked chicken breast

- 3 (15 ounce) cans white beans

- 1 cup shredded Monterey Jack cheese

DIRECTIONS

1. Heat the oil in a large saucepan over medium-low heat. Slowly cook and stir the onion until tender. Mix in the garlic, jalapeno, green chile peppers, cumin, oregano and cayenne. Continue to cook and stir the mixture until tender, about 3 minutes. Mix in the chicken broth, chicken and white beans. Simmer 15 minutes, stirring occasionally.
2. Remove the mixture from heat. Slowly stir in the cheese until melted. Serve warm.

SLOW COOKER TACO SOUP

Servings: 8 | Prep: 10m | Cooks: 8h | Total: 8h10m

NUTRITION FACTS

Calories: 361.8 | Carbohydrates: 37.8g | Protein: 18.2g | Cholesterol: 48.5mg | Sodium: 1356mg

INGREDIENTS

- 1 pound ground beef
- 1 onion, chopped
- 1 (16 ounce) can chili beans, with liquid
- 1 (8 ounce) can tomato sauce
- 2 cups water
- 2 (14.5 ounce) cans peeled and diced tomatoes

- 1 (15 ounce) can kidney beans with liquid
- 1 (15 ounce) can whole kernel corn, with liquid
- 1 (4 ounce) can diced green chile peppers
- 1 (1.25 ounce) package taco seasoning mix

DIRECTIONS

1. In a medium skillet, cook the ground beef until browned over medium heat. Drain, and set aside.
2. Place the ground beef, onion, chili beans, kidney beans, corn, tomato sauce, water, diced tomatoes, green chile peppers and taco seasoning mix in a slow cooker. Mix to blend, and cook on Low setting for 8 hours.

SIMPLE TURKEY CHILI

Servings: 8 | Prep: 15m | Cooks: 45m | Total: 1h

NUTRITION FACTS

Calories: 185 | Carbohydrates: 18.8g | Protein: 16.4g | Cholesterol: 41.8mg | Sodium: 450.3mg

INGREDIENTS

- 1 1/2 teaspoons olive oil
- 1 pound ground turkey
- 1 onion, chopped
- 2 cups water
- 1 (28 ounce) can canned crushed tomatoes
- 1 (16 ounce) can canned kidney beans -
- 2 tablespoons chili powder
- 1/2 teaspoon paprika
- 1/2 teaspoon dried oregano
- 1/2 teaspoon ground cayenne pepper
- 1/2 teaspoon ground cumin
- 1/2 teaspoon salt

- drained, rinsed, and mashed

- 1 tablespoon garlic, minced

- 1/2 teaspoon ground black pepper

DIRECTIONS

1. Heat the oil in a large pot over medium heat. Place turkey in the pot, and cook until evenly brown. Stir in onion, and cook until tender.
2. Pour water into the pot. Mix in tomatoes, kidney beans, and garlic. Season chili powder, paprika, oregano, cayenne pepper, cumin, salt, and pepper. Bring to a boil. Reduce heat to low, cover, and simmer 30 minutes.

HUMMUS

Servings: 16 | Prep: 10m | Cooks: 0m | Total: 10m

NUTRITION FACTS

Calories: 77 | Carbohydrates: 8.1g | Fat: 4.3g | Protein: 2.6g | Cholesterol: 0mg | Sodium: 236mg

INGREDIENTS

- 2 cups canned garbanzo beans, drained

- 2 cloves garlic, halved

- ⅓ cup tahini
- 1/4 cup lemon juice
- 1 teaspoon salt
- 1 tablespoon olive oil
- 1 pinch paprika
- 1 teaspoon minced fresh parsley

DIRECTIONS

1. Place the garbanzo beans, tahini, lemon juice, salt and garlic in a blender or food processor. Blend until smooth. Transfer mixture to a serving bowl.
2. Drizzle olive oil over the garbanzo bean mixture. Sprinkle with paprika and parsley.

DELICIOUS BLACK BEAN BURRITOS
Servings: 2 | Prep: 10m | Cooks: 15m | Total: 25m

NUTRITION FACTS

Calories: 692 | Carbohydrates: 70.2g | Fat: 35.8g | Protein: 21.2g | Cholesterol: 47mg | Sodium: 1803mg

INGREDIENTS

- 2 (10 inch) flour tortillas
- 1 (15 ounce) can black beans, rinsed and drained

- 2 tablespoons vegetable oil

- 1 small onion, chopped

- 1/2 red bell pepper, chopped

- 1 teaspoon minced garlic

- 1 teaspoon minced jalapeno peppers

- 3 ounces cream cheese

- 1/2 teaspoon salt

- 2 tablespoons chopped fresh cilantro

DIRECTIONS

1. Wrap tortillas in foil and place in oven heated to 350 degrees F (175 degrees C). Bake for 15 minutes or until heated through.
2. Heat oil in a 10-inch skillet over medium heat. Place onion, bell pepper, garlic and jalapenos in skillet, cook for 2 minutes stirring occasionally. Pour beans into skillet, cook 3 minutes stirring.
3. Cut cream cheese into cubes and add to skillet with salt. Cook for 2 minutes stirring occasionally. Stir cilantro into mixture.
4. Spoon mixture evenly down center of warmed tortilla and roll tortillas up. Serve immediately.

SIX CAN CHICKEN TORTILLA SOUP

Servings: 6 | Prep: 5m | Cooks: 15m | Total: 20m

NUTRITION FACTS

Calories: 214.2 | Carbohydrates: 27.2g | Protein: 17.2g | Cholesterol: 32mg | Sodium: 1482.5mg

INGREDIENTS

- 1 (15 ounce) can whole kernel corn, drained
- 1 (15 ounce) can black beans
- 2 (14.5 ounce) cans chicken broth
- 1 (10 ounce) can diced tomatoes with green chile peppers, drained
- 1 (10 ounce) can chunk chicken

DIRECTIONS

1. Open the cans of corn, chicken broth, chunk chicken, black beans, and diced tomatoes with green chilies. Pour everything into a large saucepan or stock pot. Simmer over medium heat until chicken is heated through.

THE BEST VEGETARIAN CHILI IN THE WORLD

Servings: 8 | Prep: 15m | Cooks: 1h | Total: 1h15m

NUTRITION FACTS

Calories: 390.6 | Carbohydrates: 58.7g | Protein: 28.2g | Cholesterol: 0mg | Sodium: 2571.2mg

INGREDIENTS

- 1 tablespoon olive oil
- 1/2 medium onion, chopped
- 2 bay leaves
- 1 teaspoon ground cumin
- 2 (4 ounce) cans chopped green chile peppers, drained
- 2 (12 ounce) packages vegetarian burger crumbles
- 3 (28 ounce) cans whole peeled tomatoes, crushed
- 1/4 cup chili powder

- 2 tablespoons dried oregano
- 1 tablespoon salt
- 2 stalks celery, chopped
- 2 green bell peppers, chopped
- 2 jalapeno peppers, chopped
- 3 cloves garlic, chopped
- 1 tablespoon ground black pepper
- 1 (15 ounce) can kidney beans, drained
- 1 (15 ounce) can garbanzo beans, drained
- 1 (15 ounce) can black beans
- 1 (15 ounce) can whole kernel corn

DIRECTIONS

1. Heat the olive oil in a large pot over medium heat. Stir in the onion, and season with bay leaves, cumin, oregano, and salt. Cook and stir until onion is tender, then mix in the celery, green bell peppers, jalapeno peppers, garlic, and green chile peppers. When vegetables are heated through, mix in the

vegetarian burger crumbles. Reduce heat to low, cover pot, and simmer 5 minutes.
2. Mix the tomatoes into the pot. Season chili with chili powder and pepper. Stir in the kidney beans, garbanzo beans, and black beans. Bring to a boil, reduce heat to low, and simmer 45 minutes. Stir in the corn, and continue cooking 5 minutes before serving.

BLACK BEAN AND SALSA SOUP
Servings: 4 | Prep: 10m | Cooks: 10m | Total: 20m

NUTRITION FACTS

Calories: 240 | Carbohydrates: 34.5g | Fat: 5g | Protein: 13.3g | Cholesterol: 6mg | Sodium: 1216mg

INGREDIENTS

- 2 (15 ounce) cans black beans, drained and rinsed
- 1 1/2 cups vegetable broth
- 1 cup chunky salsa
- 1 teaspoon ground cumin
- 4 tablespoons sour cream
- 2 tablespoons thinly sliced green onion

DIRECTIONS

1. In an electric food processor or blender, combine beans, broth, salsa, and cumin. Blend until fairly smooth.
2. Heat the bean mixture in a saucepan over medium heat until thoroughly heated.
3. Ladle soup into 4 individual bowls, and top each bowl with 1 tablespoon of the sour cream and 1/2 tablespoon green onion.

BLACK BEAN AND CORN QUESADILLAS

Servings: 8 | Prep: 10m | Cooks: 30m | Total: 40m

NUTRITION FACTS

Calories: 363 | Carbohydrates: 45.6g | Fat: 14.5g | Protein: 13.9g | Cholesterol: 26mg | Sodium: 732mg

INGREDIENTS

- 2 teaspoons olive oil
- 3 tablespoons finely chopped onion
- 1 (15.5 ounce) can black beans, drained and rinsed
- 1/4 cup salsa
- 1/4 teaspoon red pepper flakes
- 2 tablespoons butter, divided
- 8 (8 inch) flour tortillas

- 1 (10 ounce) can whole kernel corn, drained

- 1 tablespoon brown sugar

- 1 1/2 cups shredded Monterey Jack cheese, divided

DIRECTIONS

1. Heat oil in a large saucepan over medium heat. Stir in onion, and cook until softened, about 2 minutes. Stir in beans and corn, then add sugar, salsa, and pepper flakes; mix well. Cook until heated through, about 3 minutes.
2. Melt 2 teaspoons of the butter in a large skillet over medium heat. Place a tortilla in the skillet, sprinkle evenly with cheese, then top with some of the bean mixture. Place another tortilla on top, cook until golden, then flip and cook on the other side. Melt more butter as needed, and repeat with remaining tortillas and filling.

BLACK BEAN AND CORN SALAD

Servings: 6 | Prep: 25m | Cooks: 0m | Total: 25m

NUTRITION FACTS

Calories: 390.8 | Carbohydrates: 35.1g | Protein: 10.5g | Cholesterol: 0mg | Sodium: 829.7mg

INGREDIENTS

- 1/3 cup fresh lime juice
- 1/2 cup olive oil
- 1 clove garlic, minced
- 1 teaspoon salt
- 1/8 teaspoon ground cayenne pepper
- 2 (15 ounce) cans black beans, rinsed and drained
- 1 1/2 cups frozen corn kernels
- 1 avocado - peeled, pitted and diced
- 1 red bell pepper, chopped
- 2 tomatoes, chopped
- 6 green onions, thinly sliced
- 1/2 cup chopped fresh cilantro

DIRECTIONS

1. Place lime juice, olive oil, garlic, salt, and cayenne pepper in a small jar. Cover with lid, and shake until ingredients are well mixed.
2. In a salad bowl, combine beans, corn, avocado, bell pepper, tomatoes, green onions, and cilantro. Shake lime dressing, and pour it over the salad. Stir salad to coat vegetables and beans with dressing, and serve.

CHILI
Servings: 8 | Prep: 20m | Cooks: 2h | Total: 2h20m

NUTRITION FACTS

Calories: 532.4 | Carbohydrates: 65.3g | Protein: 32.4g | Cholesterol: 57mg | Sodium: 1413.6mg

INGREDIENTS

- 2 tablespoons vegetable oil
- 2 onions, chopped
- 3 cloves garlic, minced
- 1 pound ground beef
- 3/4 pound beef sirloin, cubed
- 1 (14 ounce) can beef broth
- 1/2 cup packed brown sugar
- 3 1/2 tablespoons chili powder
- 1 tablespoon cumin seeds
- 1 tablespoon unsweetened cocoa powder

- 1 (14.5 ounce) can peeled and diced tomatoes with juice

- 1 (12 fluid ounce) can or bottle dark beer

- 1 cup strong brewed coffee

- 2 (6 ounce) cans tomato past

- 1 teaspoon dried oregano

- 1 teaspoon ground cayenne pepper

- 1 teaspoon ground coriander

- 1 teaspoon salt

DIRECTIONS

1. Heat oil in a large saucepan over medium heat. Cook onions, garlic, ground beef and cubed sirloin in oil for 10 minutes, or until the meat is well browned and the onions are tender.
2. Mix in the diced tomatoes with juice, dark beer, coffee, tomato paste and beef broth. Season with brown sugar, chili powder, cumin, cocoa powder, oregano, cayenne pepper, coriander and salt. Stir in 2 cans of the beans and hot chile peppers. Reduce heat to low, and simmer for 1 1/2 hours.
3. Stir in the 2 remaining cans of beans, and simmer for another 30 minutes.

LAURA'S QUICK SLOW COOKER TURKEY CHILI

Servings: 8 | Prep: 15m | Cooks: 4h | Total: 4h15m

NUTRITION FACTS

Calories: 276 | Carbohydrates: 32.8g | Fat: 7.6g | Protein: 21.2g | Cholesterol: 42mg | Sodium: 547mg

INGREDIENTS

- 1 tablespoon vegetable oil
- 1 pound ground turkey
- 2 (10.75 ounce) cans low sodium tomato soup
- 2 (15 ounce) cans kidney beans, drained
- 1 (15 ounce) can black beans, drained
- 1 teaspoon red pepper flakes
- 1/2 tablespoon garlic powder
- 1/2 tablespoon ground cumin
- 1 pinch ground black pepper
- 1 pinch ground allspice

- 1/2 medium onion, chopped
- salt to taste
- 2 tablespoons chili powder

DIRECTIONS

1. Heat the oil in a skillet over medium heat. Place turkey in the skillet, and cook until evenly brown; drain.
2. Coat the inside of a slow cooker with cooking spray, and mix in turkey, tomato soup, kidney beans, black beans and onion. Season with chili powder, red pepper flakes, garlic powder, cumin, black pepper, allspice and salt.
3. Cover, and cook 8 hours on Low or 4 hours on High.

SOUTHWESTERN EGG ROLLS
Servings: 5 | Prep: 20m | Cooks: 12m | Total: 4h32m | Additional: 4h

NUTRITION FACTS

Calories: 419.2 | Carbohydrates: 21.8g | Protein: 13.6g | Cholesterol: 28.8mg | Sodium: 575.1mg

INGREDIENTS

- 2 tablespoons vegetable oil
- 1 skinless, boneless chicken breast half
- 2 tablespoons minced green onion
- 2 tablespoons minced red bell pepper
- 1/3 cup frozen corn kernels
- 1/4 cup black beans, rinsed and drained
- 1/2 tablespoon minced fresh parsley
- 1/2 teaspoon ground cumin
- 1/2 teaspoon chili powder
- 1/3 teaspoon salt
- 1 pinch ground cayenne pepper
- 3/4 cup shredded Monterey Jack cheese

- 2 tablespoons frozen chopped spinach, thawed and drained
- 5 (6 inch) flour tortillas
- 2 tablespoons diced jalapeno peppers
- 1 quart oil for deep frying

DIRECTIONS

1. Rub 1 tablespoon vegetable oil over chicken breast. In a medium saucepan over medium heat, cook chicken approximately 5 minutes per side, until meat is no longer pink and juices run clear. Remove from heat and set aside.
2. Heat remaining 1 tablespoon vegetable oil in a medium saucepan over medium heat. Stir in green onion and red pepper. Cook and stir 5 minutes, until tender.
3. Dice chicken and mix into the pan with onion and red pepper. Mix in corn, black beans, spinach, jalapeno peppers, parsley, cumin, chili powder, salt and cayenne pepper. Cook and stir 5 minutes, until well blended and tender. Remove from heat and stir in Monterey Jack cheese so that it melts.
4. Wrap tortillas with a clean, lightly moist cloth. Microwave on high approximately 1 minute, or until hot and pliable.
5. Spoon even amounts of the mixture into each tortilla. Fold ends of tortillas, then roll tightly around mixture. Secure with toothpicks. Arrange in a medium dish, cover with plastic, and place in the freezer. Freeze at least 4 hours.
6. In a large, deep skillet, heat oil for deep frying to 375 degrees F (190 degrees C). Deep fry frozen, stuffed tortillas 10

minutes each, or until dark golden brown. Drain on paper towels before serving.

SPICY BEAN SALSA
Servings: 12 | Prep: 10m | Cooks: 8h | Total: 8h10m | Additional: 8h

NUTRITION FACTS

Calories: 155 | Carbohydrates: 20.4g | Protein: 5g | Cholesterol: 0mg | Sodium: 948.9mg

INGREDIENTS

- 1 (15 ounce) can black-eyed peas
- 1 (15 ounce) can black beans, rinsed and drained
- 1 (15 ounce) can whole kernel corn, drained
- 1/2 cup chopped onion
- 1 (4 ounce) can diced jalapeno peppers
- 1 (14.5 ounce) can diced tomatoes, drained
- 1 cup Italian-style salad dressing
- 1/2 teaspoon garlic salt

- 1/2 cup chopped green bell pepper

DIRECTIONS

1. In a medium bowl, combine black-eyed peas, black beans, corn, onion, green bell pepper, jalapeno peppers and tomatoes. Season with Italian-style salad dressing and garlic salt; mix well. Cover, and refrigerate overnight to blend flavors.

SEAN'S FALAFEL AND CUCUMBER SAUCE

Servings: 4 | Prep: 20m | Cooks: 10m | Total: 1h | Additional: 30m

NUTRITION FACTS

Calories: 586 | Carbohydrates: 59.5g | Protein: 14.7g | Cholesterol: 50.3mg | Sodium: 1580.1mg

INGREDIENTS

- 1 (6 ounce) container plain yogurt
- 1 teaspoon ground coriander
- 1/2 cucumber - peeled, seeded, and finely chopped
- 1 teaspoon salt

- 1 teaspoon dried dill weed
- 1/2 teaspoon salt and pepper to taste
- 1 tablespoon mayonnaise
- 1 (15 ounce) can chickpeas (garbanzo beans), drained
- 1 onion, chopped
- 1/2 cup fresh parsley
- 2 cloves garlic, chopped
- 1 egg

- 1 dash pepper
- 1 pinch cayenne pepper
- 1 teaspoon lemon juice
- 1 teaspoon baking powder
- 1 tablespoon olive oil
- 1 cup dry bread crumbs
- 1 quart oil for frying
- 2 eaches pita breads, cut in half

- 2 teaspoons ground cumin
- 1 cup chopped tomatoes

DIRECTIONS

1. In a small bowl combine yogurt, cucumber, dill, salt, pepper and mayonnaise and mix well. Chill for at least 30 minutes.
2. In a large bowl mash chickpeas until thick and pasty; don't use a blender, as the consistency will be too thin. In a blender, process onion, parsley and garlic until smooth. Stir into mashed chickpeas.
3. In a small bowl combine egg, cumin, coriander, salt, pepper, cayenne, lemon juice and baking powder. Stir into chickpea mixture along with olive oil. Slowly add bread crumbs until mixture is not sticky but will hold together; add more or less bread crumbs, as needed. Form 8 balls and then flatten into patties.
4. Heat 1 inch of oil in a large skillet over medium-high heat. Fry patties in hot oil until brown on both sides. Serve two falafels in each pita half topped with chopped tomatoes and cucumber sauce.

ZESTY QUINOA SALAD

Servings: 6 | Prep: 20m | Cooks: 10m | Total: 30m

NUTRITION FACTS

Calories: 269.6 | Carbohydrates: 33.8g | Protein: 8.9g | Cholesterol: 0mg | Sodium: 674.5mg

INGREDIENTS

- 1 cup quinoa

- 2 cups water

- 1/4 cup extra-virgin olive oil

- 2 limes, juiced

- 2 teaspoons ground cumin

- 1 teaspoon salt

- 1/2 teaspoon red pepper flakes, or more to taste

- 1 1/2 cups halved cherry tomatoes

- 1 (15 ounce) can black beans, drained and rinsed

- 5 green onions, finely chopped

- 1/4 cup chopped fresh cilantro

- 1 pinch salt and ground black pepper to taste

DIRECTIONS

1. Bring quinoa and water to a boil in a saucepan. Reduce heat to medium-low, cover, and simmer until quinoa is tender and water has been absorbed, 10 to 15 minutes. Set aside to cool.

2. Whisk olive oil, lime juice, cumin, 1 teaspoon salt, and red pepper flakes together in a bowl.
3. Combine quinoa, tomatoes, black beans, and green onions together in a bowl. Pour dressing over quinoa mixture; toss to coat. Stir in cilantro; season with salt and black pepper. Serve immediately or chill in refrigerator.

BLACK BEAN AND COUSCOUS SALAD

Servings: 8 | Prep: 30m | Cooks: 0m | Total: 35m | Additional: 5m

NUTRITION FACTS

Calories: 253 | Carbohydrates: 51.1g | Fat: 5.8g | Protein: 10.3g | Cholesterol: 0mg | Sodium: 415mg

INGREDIENTS

- 1 cup uncooked couscous
- 1 1/4 cups chicken broth
- 3 tablespoons extra virgin olive oil
- 8 green onions, chopped
- 1 red bell pepper, seeded and chopped
- 1/4 cup chopped fresh cilantro

- 2 tablespoons fresh lime juice
- 1 teaspoon red wine vinegar
- 1/2 teaspoon ground cumin
- 1 cup frozen corn kernels, thawed
- 2 (15 ounce) cans black beans, drained
- salt and pepper to taste

DIRECTIONS

1. Bring chicken broth to a boil in a 2 quart or larger sauce pan and stir in the couscous. Cover the pot and remove from heat. Let stand for 5 minutes.
2. In a large bowl, whisk together the olive oil, lime juice, vinegar and cumin. Add green onions, red pepper, cilantro, corn and beans and toss to coat.
3. Fluff the couscous well, breaking up any chunks. Add to the bowl with the vegetables and mix well. Season with salt and pepper to taste and serve at once or refrigerate until ready to serve.

RED LENTIL CURRY

Servings: 8 | Prep: 10m | Cooks: 30m | Total: 40m

NUTRITION FACTS

Calories: 192 | Carbohydrates: 32.5g | Fat: 2.6g | Protein: 12.1g | Cholesterol: 0mg | Sodium: 572mg

INGREDIENTS

- 2 cups red lentils
- 1 large onion, diced
- 1 tablespoon vegetable oil
- 2 tablespoons curry paste
- 1 tablespoon curry powder
- 1 teaspoon ground turmeric
- 1 teaspoon ground cumin
- 1 teaspoon chili powder
- 1 teaspoon salt
- 1 teaspoon white sugar
- 1 teaspoon minced garlic
- 1 teaspoon minced fresh ginger
- 1 (14.25 ounce) can tomato puree

DIRECTIONS

1. Wash the lentils in cold water until the water runs clear. Put lentils in a pot with enough water to cover; bring to a boil,

place a cover on the pot, reduce heat to medium-low, and simmer, adding water during cooking as needed to keep covered, until tender, 15 to 20 minutes. Drain.
2. Heat vegetable oil in a large skillet over medium heat; cook and stir onions in hot oil until caramelized, about 20 minutes.
3. Mix curry paste, curry powder, turmeric, cumin, chili powder, salt, sugar, garlic, and ginger together in a large bowl; stir into the onions. Increase heat to high and cook, stirring constantly, until fragrant, 1 to 2 minutes.
4. Stir in the tomato puree, remove from heat and stir into the lentils.

SPICY BLACK BEAN VEGETABLE SOUP

Servings: 8 | Prep: 15m | Cooks: 35m | Total: 50m

NUTRITION FACTS

Calories: 164 | Carbohydrates: 26.9g | Fat: 3.4g | Protein: 7.6g | Cholesterol: 26.9mg | Sodium: 683mg

INGREDIENTS

- 1 tablespoon vegetable oil
- 1 onion, chopped
- 1 clove garlic, minced
- 2 carrots, chopped
- 2 teaspoons chili powder
- 1 teaspoon ground cumin
- 4 cups vegetable stock
- 2 (15 ounce) cans black beans, rinsed and drained
- 1 (8.75 ounce) can whole kernel corn
- 1/4 teaspoon ground black pepper
- 1 (14.5 ounce) can stewed tomatoes

DIRECTIONS

1. In large saucepan, heat oil over medium heat; cook onion, garlic, and carrots, stirring occasionally, for 5 minutes or until onion is softened. Add chili powder and cumin; cook, stirring,

for 1 minute. Add stock, 1 can of the beans, corn, and pepper; bring to boil.

2. Meanwhile, in food processor or blender, puree together tomatoes and remaining can of beans; add to pot. Reduce heat, cover, and simmer for 10 to 15 minutes or until carrots are tender.

BOSTON BAKED BEANS
Servings: 6 | Prep: 30m | Cooks: 4h | Total: 5h | Additional: 30m

NUTRITION FACTS

Calories: 382 | Carbohydrates: 63.1g | Fat: 6.3g | Protein: 20.7g | Cholesterol: 14mg | Sodium: 1320mg

INGREDIENTS

- 2 cups navy beans
- 1/2 pound bacon
- 1 onion, finely diced
- 3 tablespoons molasses
- 1/4 teaspoon ground black pepper
- 1/4 teaspoon dry mustard
- 1/2 cup ketchup
- 1 tablespoon Worcestershire sauce

2 • teaspoons salt   1/4 cup brown sugar

DIRECTIONS

1. Soak beans overnight in cold water. Simmer the beans in the same water until tender, approximately 1 to 2 hours. Drain and reserve the liquid.
2. Preheat oven to 325 degrees F (165 degrees C).
3. Arrange the beans in a 2 quart bean pot or casserole dish by placing a portion of the beans in the bottom of dish, and layering them with bacon and onion.
4. In a saucepan, combine molasses, salt, pepper, dry mustard, ketchup, Worcestershire sauce and brown sugar. Bring the mixture to a boil and pour over beans. Pour in just enough of the reserved bean water to cover the beans. Cover the dish with a lid or aluminum foil.
5. Bake for 3 to 4 hours in the preheated oven, until beans are tender. Remove the lid about halfway through cooking, and add more liquid if necessary to prevent the beans from getting too dry.

WHITE BEAN CHICKEN CHILI

Servings: 9 | Prep: 10m | Cooks: 25m | Total: 35m

NUTRITION FACTS

Calories: 219.8 | Carbohydrates: 21.2g | Protein: 20.1g | Cholesterol: 39.8mg | Sodium: 785.6mg

INGREDIENTS

- 2 tablespoons vegetable oil
- 1/2 teaspoon dried oregano

- 1 onion, chopped
- 2 cloves garlic, minced
- 1 (14.5 ounce) can chicken broth
- 1 (18.75 ounce) can tomatillos, drained and chopped
- 1 (16 ounce) can diced tomatoes
- 1 (7 ounce) can diced green chiles
- 1/2 teaspoon ground coriander seed
- 1/4 teaspoon ground cumin
- 2 ears fresh corn
- 1 pound diced, cooked chicken meat
- 1 (15 ounce) can white beans
- 1 pinch salt and black pepper to taste

DIRECTIONS

1. Heat oil, and cook onion and garlic until soft.
2. Stir in broth, tomatillos, tomatoes, chilies, and spices. Bring to a boil, then simmer for 10 minutes.
3. Add corn, chicken, and beans; simmer 5 minutes. Season with salt and pepper to taste.

AUTHENTIC LOUISIANA RED BEANS AND RICE

Servings: 8 | Prep: 25m | Cooks: 3h5m | Total: 11h30m | Additional: 8h

NUTRITION FACTS

Calories: 630.4 | Carbohydrates: 79.1g | Protein: 24g | Cholesterol: 32.9mg | Sodium: 630.9mg

INGREDIENTS

- 1 pound dry kidney beans
- 1/4 cup olive oil
- 1 large onion, chopped
- 1 green bell pepper, chopped
- 2 tablespoons minced garlic
- 1/2 teaspoon cayenne pepper
- 1 teaspoon dried thyme
- 1/4 teaspoon dried sage
- 1 tablespoon dried parsley
- 1 teaspoon Cajun seasoning

- 2 stalks celery, chopped
- 6 cups water
- 2 eaches bay leaves
- 1 pound andouille sausage, sliced
- 4 cups water
- 2 cups long grain white rice

DIRECTIONS

1. Rinse beans, and then soak in a large pot of water overnight.
2. In a skillet, heat oil over medium heat. Cook onion, bell pepper, garlic, and celery in olive oil for 3 to 4 minutes.
3. Rinse beans, and transfer to a large pot with 6 cups water. Stir cooked vegetables into beans. Season with bay leaves, cayenne pepper, thyme, sage, parsley, and Cajun seasoning. Bring to a boil, and then reduce heat to medium-low. Simmer for 2 1/2 hours.
4. Stir sausage into beans, and continue to simmer for 30 minutes.
5. Meanwhile, prepare the rice. In a saucepan, bring water and rice to a boil. Reduce heat, cover, and simmer for 20 minutes. Serve beans over steamed white rice.

WHITE CHILI WITH GROUND TURKEY
Servings: 8 | Prep: 15m | Cooks: 30m | Total: 45m

NUTRITION FACTS

Calories: 396 | Carbohydrates: 26.7g | Fat: 17.3g | Protein: 31.5g | Cholesterol: 92mg | Sodium: 1366mg

INGREDIENTS

- 1 onion, chopped
- 3 cloves garlic, minced
- 1 1/2 pounds ground turkey
- 2 (4 ounce) cans canned green chile peppers, chopped
- 1 tablespoon ground cumin
- 1 tablespoon dried oregano
- 1 teaspoon ground cinnamon
- ground cayenne pepper to taste
- ground white pepper to taste
- 3 (15 ounce) cans cannellini beans
- 5 cups chicken broth
- 2 cups shredded Monterey Jack cheese

DIRECTIONS

1. In a large pot over medium heat, combine the onion, garlic and ground turkey and saute for 10 minutes, or until turkey is well browned. Add the chile peppers, cumin, oregano, cinnamon, cayenne pepper to taste and white pepper to taste and saute for 5 more minutes.
2. Add two cans of the beans and the chicken broth to the pot. Take the third can of beans and puree them in a blender or food processor. Add this to the pot along with the cheese. Stir well and simmer for 10 minutes, allowing the cheese to melt.

BLACK BEANS AND RICE

Servings: 10 | Prep: 5m | Cooks: 25m | Total: 30m

NUTRITION FACTS

Calories: 140.4 | Carbohydrates: 27.1g | Protein: 6.3g | Cholesterol: 354.4mg | Sodium: 354mg

INGREDIENTS

- 1 teaspoon olive oil
- 1 onion, chopped
- 2 cloves garlic, minced
- 1 1/2 cups low sodium, low fat vegetable broth
- 1 teaspoon ground cumin
- 1/4 teaspoon cayenne pepper

- 3/4 cup uncooked white rice
- 3 1/2 cups canned black beans, drained

DIRECTIONS

1. In a stockpot over medium-high heat, heat the oil. Add the onion and garlic and saute for 4 minutes. Add the rice and saute for 2 minutes.
2. Add the vegetable broth, bring to a boil, cover and lower the heat and cook for 20 minutes. Add the spices and black beans.

SWEET POTATO, CARROT, APPLE, AND RED LENTIL SOUP

Servings: 6 | Prep: 20m | Cooks: 50m | Total: 1h10m

NUTRITION FACTS

Calories: 321.6 | Carbohydrates: 52.9g | Protein: 9g | Cholesterol: 21.6mg | Sodium: 876.3mg

INGREDIENTS

- 1/4 cup butter
- 2 large sweet potatoes, peeled and chopped
- 3 large carrots, peeled and chopped
- 1/2 teaspoon ground black pepper
- 1 teaspoon salt
- 1/2 teaspoon ground cumin

- 1 apple, peeled, cored and chopped
- 1 onion, chopped
- 1/2 cup red lentils
- 1/2 teaspoon minced fresh ginger
- 1/2 teaspoon chili powder
- 1/2 teaspoon paprika
- 4 cups vegetable broth
- 1/2 cup plain yogurt

DIRECTIONS

1. Melt the butter in a large, heavy bottomed pot over medium-high heat. Place the chopped sweet potatoes, carrots, apple, and onion in the pot. Stir and cook the apples and vegetables until the onions are translucent, about 10 minutes.
2. Stir the lentils, ginger, ground black pepper, salt, cumin, chili powder, paprika, and vegetable broth into the pot with the apple and vegetable mixture. Bring the soup to a boil over high heat, then reduce the heat to medium-low, cover, and simmer until the lentils and vegetables are soft, about 30 minutes.
3. Working in batches, pour the soup into a blender, filling the pitcher no more than halfway full. Hold down the lid of the blender with a folded kitchen towel, and carefully start the blender, using a few quick pulses to get the soup moving before leaving it on to puree. Puree in batches until smooth

and pour into a clean pot. Alternately, you can use a stick blender and puree the soup right in the cooking pot.
4. Return the pureed soup to the cooking pot. Bring back to a simmer over medium-high heat, about 10 minutes. Add water as needed to thin the soup to your preferred consistency. Serve with yogurt for garnish.

BASIC HAM AND BEAN SOUP
Servings: 9 | Prep: 30m | Cooks: 2h30m | Total: 3h

NUTRITION FACTS

Calories: 256.9 | Carbohydrates: 29g | Protein: 18.1g | Cholesterol: 30mg | Sodium: 771.4mg

INGREDIENTS

- 1 pound dry great Northern beans
- 8 cups water
- 1/2 teaspoon salt
- 1 ham hock
- 1 cup chopped onion
- 1 teaspoon minced garlic
- 1 teaspoon mustard powder
- 2 eaches bay leaves

- 1 cup chopped carrots
- 2 cups chopped ham
- 1/2 stalk celery, chopped
- 1/2 teaspoon ground white pepper

DIRECTIONS

1. Rinse the beans, sorting out any broken or discolored ones. In a large pot over high heat, bring the water to a boil. Add the salt and the beans and remove from heat. Let beans sit in the hot water for at least 60 minutes.
2. After the 60 minutes of soaking, return the pot to high heat and place the ham bone, carrots, celery, onion, garlic, mustard and bay leaves in the pot. Stir well, bring to a boil, reduce heat to low and simmer for 60 more minutes.
3. Remove ham bone and discard. Stir in the chopped ham and simmer for 30 more minutes. Season with ground white pepper to taste.

CREAMY WHITE CHILI

Servings: 8 | Prep: 15m | Cooks: 40m | Total: 55m

NUTRITION FACTS

Calories: 334.4 | Carbohydrates: 29.7g | Protein: 21.3g | Cholesterol: 63.4mg | Sodium: 887.7mg

INGREDIENTS

- 1 tablespoon olive oil
- 1 pound skinless, boneless chicken breast halves, cut into 1/2-inch cubes
- 1 onion, chopped
- 2 cloves garlic, chopped
- 2 (15.5 ounce) cans great Northern beans, rinsed and drained
- 1 teaspoon salt
- 1 teaspoon ground cumin
- 1 teaspoon dried oregano
- 1/2 teaspoon ground black pepper
- 1/4 teaspoon cayenne pepper
- 1 cup sour cream

- 1 (14.5 ounce) can chicken broth

- 2 (4 ounce) cans chopped green chiles
- 1/2 cup heavy whipping cream

DIRECTIONS

1. Heat olive oil in a large saucepan over medium heat; cook and stir chicken, onion, and garlic into the hot oil until chicken is no longer pink in the center and the juices run clear, 10 to 15 minutes.
2. Mix Great Northern beans, chicken broth, green chiles, salt, cumin, oregano, black pepper, and cayenne pepper into chicken mixture; bring to a boil. Reduce heat and simmer until flavors have blended, about 30 minutes.
3. Remove chili from heat; stir in sour cream and whipping cream until incorporated.

QUINOA BLACK BEAN BURGERS

Servings: 5 | Prep: 15m | Cooks: 20m | Total: 35m

NUTRITION FACTS

Calories: 245 | Carbohydrates: 28.9g | Fat: 10.6g | Protein: 9.3g | Cholesterol: 37mg | Sodium: 679mg

INGREDIENTS

- 1 (15 ounce) can black beans, rinsed and drained
- 1/4 cup quinoa
- 1/2 cup water
- 1/2 cup bread crumbs
- 1/4 cup minced yellow bell pepper
- 2 tablespoons minced onion
- 1 large clove garlic, minced
- 1 1/2 teaspoons ground cumin
- 1/2 teaspoon salt
- 1 teaspoon hot pepper sauce (such as Frank's RedHot®)
- 1 egg
- 3 tablespoons olive oil

DIRECTIONS

1. Bring the quinoa and water to a boil in a saucepan. Reduce heat to medium-low, cover, and simmer until the quinoa is

tender and the water has been absorbed, about 15 to 20 minutes.
2. Roughly mash the black beans with a fork leaving some whole black beans in a paste-like mixture.
3. Mix the quinoa, bread crumbs, bell pepper, onion, garlic, cumin, salt, hot pepper sauce, and egg into the black beans using your hands.
4. Form the black bean mixture into 5 patties.
5. Heat the olive oil in a large skillet.
6. Cook the patties in the hot oil until heated through, 2 to 3 minutes per side.

MEXICAN CASSEROLE

Servings: 5 | Prep: 15m | Cooks: 15m | Total: 30m

NUTRITION FACTS

Calories: 383.7 | Carbohydrates: 34g | Protein: 26.8g | Cholesterol: 59.1mg | Sodium: 1286.4mg

INGREDIENTS

- 2 tablespoons vegetable oil
- 3/4 pound cubed skinless, boneless chicken breast meat
- 1/2 (1.25 ounce) package taco
- 1/4 cup salsa
- water as needed
- 1 cup shredded Mexican-style cheese

seasoning mix

- 1 (15 ounce) can black beans, rinsed and drained
- 1 1/2 cups crushed plain tortilla chips
- 1 (8.75 ounce) can sweet corn, drained

DIRECTIONS

1. In a large skillet over medium high heat, saute chicken in oil until cooked through and no longer pink inside. Add taco seasoning, beans, corn, salsa and a little water to prevent drying out. Cover skillet and simmer over medium low heat for 10 minutes.
2. Preheat oven to 350 degrees F (175 degrees C).
3. Transfer chicken mixture to a 9x13 inch baking dish. Top with 1/2 cup of the cheese and crushed tortilla chips.
4. Bake in the preheated oven for 15 minutes. Add remaining 1/2 cup cheese and bake until cheese is melted and bubbly.

FANTASTIC BLACK BEAN CHILI
Servings: 6 | Prep: 20m | Cooks: 1h15m | Total: 1h35m

NUTRITION FACTS

Calories: 365.6 | Carbohydrates: 44.1g | Protein: 29.6g | Cholesterol: 55.8mg | Sodium: 969.2mg

INGREDIENTS

- 1 tablespoon vegetable oil
- 1 onion, diced
- 2 cloves garlic, minced
- 1 pound ground turkey
- 3 (15 ounce) cans black beans, undrained
- 1 (14.5 ounce) can crushed tomatoes
- 1 1/2 tablespoons chili powder
- 1 tablespoon dried oregano
- 1 tablespoon dried basil leaves
- 1 tablespoon red wine vinegar

DIRECTIONS

1. Heat the oil in a large heavy pot over medium heat; cook onion and garlic until onions are translucent. Add turkey and cook, stirring, until meat is brown. Stir in beans, tomatoes, chili powder, oregano, basil and vinegar. Reduce heat to low,

cover and simmer 60 minutes or more, until flavors are well blended.

BEAKER'S VEGETABLE BARLEY SOUP

Servings: 8 | Prep: 15m | Cooks: 1h30m | Total: 1h45m

NUTRITION FACTS

Calories: 188 | Carbohydrates: 37g | Protein: 6.9g | Cholesterol: 0mg | Sodium: 968.8mg

INGREDIENTS

- 2 quarts vegetable broth
- 1 cup uncooked barley
- 2 large carrots, chopped
- 2 stalks celery, chopped
- 1 (14.5 ounce) can diced tomatoes with juice
- 1 teaspoon garlic powder
- 1 teaspoon white sugar
- 1 teaspoon salt
- 1/2 teaspoon ground black pepper
- 1 teaspoon dried parsley

- 1 zucchini, chopped
- 1 (15 ounce) can garbanzo beans, drained
- 1 onion, chopped
- 3 eaches bay leaves
- 1 teaspoon curry powder
- 1 teaspoon paprika
- 1 teaspoon Worcestershire sauce

DIRECTIONS

1. Pour the vegetable broth into a large pot. Add the barley, carrots, celery, tomatoes, zucchini, garbanzo beans, onion, and bay leaves. Season with garlic powder, sugar, salt, pepper, parsley, curry powder, paprika, and Worcestershire sauce. Bring to a boil, then cover and simmer over medium-low heat for 90 minutes. The soup will be very thick. You may adjust by adding more broth or less barley if desired. Remove bay leaves before serving.

SLOW COOKER CHILI
Servings: 8 | Prep: 15m | Cooks: 8h | Total: 8h15m

NUTRITION FACTS

Calories: 272.9 | Carbohydrates: 33.4g | Protein: 18.9g | Cholesterol: 34.4mg | Sodium: 975mg

INGREDIENTS

- 1 pound ground beef
- 3/4 cup diced onion
- 3/4 cup diced celery
- 3/4 cup diced green bell pepper
- 2 cloves garlic, minced
- 2 (10.75 ounce) cans tomato puree
- 1 (15 ounce) can kidney beans with liquid
- 1 (15 ounce) can cannellini beans with liquid
- 1/2 tablespoon chili powder
- 1/2 teaspoon dried parsley
- 1 teaspoon salt
- 3/4 teaspoon dried basil
- 3/4 teaspoon dried oregano
- 1/4 teaspoon ground black pepper

- 1 (15 ounce) can kidney beans, drained
- 1/8 teaspoon hot pepper sauce

DIRECTIONS

1. Place the beef in a skillet over medium heat, and cook until evenly brown. Drain grease.
2. Place the beef in a slow cooker, and mix in onion, celery, green bell pepper, garlic, tomato puree, kidney beans, and cannellini beans. Season with chili powder, parsley, salt, basil, oregano, black pepper, and hot pepper sauce.
3. Cover, and cook 8 hours on Low.

GRANDMA'S SLOW COOKER VEGETARIAN CHILI

Servings: 8 | Prep: 10m | Cooks: 2h | Total: 2h10m

NUTRITION FACTS

Calories: 259.9 | Carbohydrates: 52.6g | Protein: 12.4g | Cholesterol: 0.8mg | Sodium: 965.9mg

INGREDIENTS

- 1 (19 ounce) can black bean soup
- 1 green bell pepper, chopped
- 1 (15 ounce) can kidney beans, rinsed
- 2 stalks celery, chopped

and drained

- 1 (15 ounce) can garbanzo beans, rinsed and drained
- 1 (16 ounce) can vegetarian baked beans
- 1 (14.5 ounce) can chopped tomatoes in puree
- 1 (15 ounce) can whole kernel corn, drained
- 1 onion, chopped
- 2 cloves garlic, chopped
- 1 tablespoon chili powder, or to taste
- 1 tablespoon dried parsley
- 1 tablespoon dried oregano
- 1 tablespoon dried basil

DIRECTIONS

1. In a slow cooker, combine black bean soup, kidney beans, garbanzo beans, baked beans, tomatoes, corn, onion, bell pepper and celery. Season with garlic, chili powder, parsley, oregano and basil. Cook for at least two hours on High.

VEGAN BLACK BEAN SOUP

Servings: 6 | Prep: 15m | Cooks: 30m | Total: 45m

NUTRITION FACTS

Calories: 410.2 | Carbohydrates: 75.3g | Protein: 21.9g | Cholesterol: 0mg | Sodium: 1733.6mg

INGREDIENTS

- 1 tablespoon olive oil
- 1 large onion, chopped
- 1 stalk celery, chopped
- 2 carrots, chopped
- 4 cloves garlic, chopped
- 2 tablespoons chili powder
- 1 tablespoon ground cumin
- 1 pinch black pepper
- 4 cups vegetable broth
- 4 (15 ounce) cans black beans
- 1 (15 ounce) can whole kernel corn
- 1 (14.5 ounce) can crushed tomatoes

DIRECTIONS

1. Heat oil in a large pot over medium-high heat. Saute onion, celery, carrots and garlic for 5 minutes. Season with chili powder, cumin, and black pepper; cook for 1 minute. Stir in vegetable broth, 2 cans of beans, and corn. Bring to a boil.
2. Meanwhile, in a food processor or blender, process remaining 2 cans beans and tomatoes until smooth. Stir into boiling soup mixture, reduce heat to medium, and simmer for 15 minutes.

GARBANZO BEAN CHOCOLATE CAKE (GLUTEN FREE!)

Servings: 12 | Prep: 15m | Cooks: 40m | Total: 1h10m | Additional: 15m

NUTRITION FACTS

Calories: 229 | Carbohydrates: 36.8g | Protein: 5.2g | Cholesterol: 62mg | Sodium: 180.4mg

INGREDIENTS

- 1 1/2 cups semisweet chocolate chips
- 1 (19 ounce) can garbanzo beans, rinsed and drained
- 4 eggs
- 3/4 cup white sugar
- 1/2 teaspoon baking powder
- 1 tablespoon confectioners' sugar

for dusting

DIRECTIONS

1. Preheat the oven to 350 degrees F (175 degrees C). Grease a 9-inch round cake pan.
2. Place the chocolate chips into a microwave-safe bowl. Cook in the microwave for about 2 minutes, stirring every 20 seconds after the first minute, until chocolate is melted and smooth. If you have a powerful microwave, reduce the power to 50 percent.
3. Combine the beans and eggs in the bowl of a food processor. Process until smooth. Add the sugar and the baking powder, and pulse to blend. Pour in the melted chocolate and blend until smooth, scraping down the corners to make sure chocolate is completely mixed. Transfer the batter to the prepared cake pan.
4. Bake for 40 minutes in the preheated oven, or until a knife inserted into the center of the cake comes out clean. Cool in the pan on a wire rack for 10 to 15 minutes before inverting onto a serving plate. Dust with confectioners' sugar just before serving.

BLACK BEAN BROWNIES
Servings: 16 | Prep: 10m | Cooks: 30m | Total: 40m

NUTRITION FACTS

Calories: 126 | Carbohydrates: 18.1g | Fat: 5.3g | Protein: 3.3g | Cholesterol: 35mg | Sodium: 129mg

INGREDIENTS

- 1 (15.5 ounce) can black beans, rinsed and drained
- 3 eggs
- 3 tablespoons vegetable oil
- 1/4 cup cocoa powder
- 1 pinch salt
- 1 teaspoon vanilla extract
- 3/4 cup white sugar
- 1 teaspoon instant coffee (optional)
- 1/2 cup milk chocolate chips (optional)

DIRECTIONS

1. Preheat oven to 350 degrees F (175 degrees C). Lightly grease an 8x8 square baking dish.
2. Combine the black beans, eggs, oil, cocoa powder, salt, vanilla extract, sugar, and instant coffee in a blender; blend until smooth; pour the mixture into the prepared baking dish. Sprinkle the chocolate chips over the top of the mixture.
3. Bake in the preheated oven until the top is dry and the edges start to pull away from the sides of the pan, about 30 minutes.

SEVEN LAYER TORTILLA PIE

Servings: 6 | Prep: 15m | Cooks: 40m | Total: 55m

NUTRITION FACTS

Calories: 405.1 | Carbohydrates: 54.8g | Protein: 21.1g | Cholesterol: 16.3mg | Sodium: 1325.3mg

INGREDIENTS

- 2 (15 ounce) cans pinto beans, drained and rinsed
- 1 cup salsa, divided
- 2 cloves garlic, minced
- 2 tablespoons chopped fresh cilantro
- 1 (15 ounce) can black beans, rinsed and drained
- 1/2 cup chopped tomatoes
- 7 (8 inch) flour tortillas
- 2 cups shredded reduced-fat Cheddar cheese
- 1 cup salsa
- 1/2 cup sour cream

DIRECTIONS

1. Preheat oven to 400 degrees F (200 degrees C).
2. In a large bowl, mash pinto beans. Stir in 3/4 cup salsa and garlic.
3. In a separate bowl, mix together 1/4 cup salsa, cilantro, black beans and tomatoes.
4. Place 1 tortilla in a pie plate or tart dish. Spread 3/4 cup pinto bean mixture over tortilla to within 1/2 inch of edge. Top with 1/4 cup cheese, and cover with another tortilla. Spread with 2/3 cup black bean mixture, and top with 1/4 cup cheese. Repeat layering twice. Cover with remaining tortilla, and spread with remaining pinto bean mixture and cheese.
5. Cover with foil, and bake in preheated oven for about 40 minutes. Cut into wedges, and serve with salsa and sour cream.

PAT'S BAKED BEANS

Servings: 10 | Prep: 15m | Cooks: 1h15m | Total: 1h30m

NUTRITION FACTS

Calories: 398.7 | Carbohydrates: 68g | Protein: 14.1g | Cholesterol: 12.5mg | Sodium: 949.9mg

INGREDIENTS

- 6 slices bacon
- 1 (15 ounce) can garbanzo beans, drained
- 1 cup chopped onion
- 3/4 cup ketchup

- 1 clove garlic, minced
- 1 (16 ounce) can pinto beans
- 1 (16 ounce) can great Northern beans, drained
- 1 (16 ounce) can baked beans
- 1 (16 ounce) can red kidney beans, drained
- 1/2 cup molasses
- 1/4 cup packed brown sugar
- 2 tablespoons Worcestershire sauce
- 1 tablespoon yellow mustard
- 1/2 teaspoon pepper

DIRECTIONS

1. Preheat oven to 375 degrees F (190 degrees C).
2. Place bacon in a large, deep skillet. Cook over medium high heat until evenly brown. Drain, reserving 2 tablespoons of drippings, crumble and set aside in a large bowl. Cook the onion and garlic in the reserved drippings until onion is tender; drain excess grease and transfer to the bowl with the bacon.
3. To the bacon and onions add pinto beans, northern beans, baked beans, kidney beans and garbanzo beans. Stir in ketchup, molasses, brown sugar, Worcestershire sauce,

mustard and black pepper. Mix well and transfer to a 9x12 inch casserole dish.
4. Cover and bake in preheated oven for 1 hour.

SLOW COOKER LENTIL AND HAM SOUP

Servings: 6 | Prep: 20m | Cooks: 11h | Total: 11h20m

NUTRITION FACTS

Calories: 222 | Carbohydrates: 26.3g | Protein: 15.1g | Cholesterol: 19.7mg | Sodium: 1169.6mg

INGREDIENTS

- 1 cup dried lentils
- 1 cup chopped celery
- 1 cup chopped carrots
- 1 cup chopped onion
- 2 cloves garlic, minced
- 1/4 teaspoon dried thyme
- 1/2 teaspoon dried oregano
- 1 bay leaf
- 1/4 teaspoon black pepper
- 32 ounces chicken broth
- 1 cup water

- 1 1/2 cups diced cooked ham

- 1/2 teaspoon dried basil
- 8 teaspoons tomato sauce

DIRECTIONS

1. In a 3 1/2 quart or larger slow cooker combine the lentils, celery, carrots, onion, garlic and ham. Season with basil, thyme, oregano, the bay leaf and pepper. Stir in the chicken broth, water and tomato sauce. Cover and cook on Low for 11 hours. Discard the bay leaf before serving.

LAYERED CHICKEN AND BLACK BEAN ENCHILADA CASSEROLE
Servings: 8 | Prep: 25m | Cooks: 45m | Total: 1h10m

NUTRITION FACTS

Calories: 366.4 | Carbohydrates: 16.4g | Protein: 23g | Cholesterol: 91.7mg | Sodium: 508.3mg

INGREDIENTS

- 2 cups diced chicken breast meat
- 1 (4.5 ounce) can diced green chile peppers, drained

- 1/2 teaspoon ground cumin
- 1/2 teaspoon ground coriander
- 2 tablespoons chopped fresh cilantro
- 1 (15 ounce) can black beans, rinsed and drained
- 1 (10 ounce) can red enchilada sauce
- 8 (6 inch) corn tortillas
- 2 cups shredded Mexican blend cheese
- 1 (8 ounce) container sour cream

DIRECTIONS

1. Preheat the oven to 375 degrees F (190 degrees C).
2. Heat a large skillet over medium heat, and spray with vegetable cooking spray. Saute chicken with cumin and coriander until chicken is cooked through. Transfer to a medium bowl. Stir in the cilantro, black beans, and green chile peppers.
3. Spread half of the enchilada sauce over the bottom of an 11x7 inch baking dish. Place 4 tortillas over the sauce, overlapping if necessary. Spoon half of the chicken mixture over the tortillas, and sprinkle with half of the cheese and half of the sour cream. Spoon the remaining enchilada sauce over the cheese, and make another layer of tortillas. Layer the remaining chicken mixture over the tortillas. Cover dish with a lid or aluminum foil.

4. Bake for 30 minutes in the preheated oven. Remove the cover, and sprinkle the remaining cheese over the top and dot with sour cream. Continue cooking, uncovered, for an additional 5 to 10 minutes, or until cheese melts. Let stand 10 minutes before serving.

BEST BLACK BEANS

Servings: 4 | Prep: 10m | Cooks: 5m | Total: 15m

NUTRITION FACTS

Calories: 112 | Carbohydrates: 20.8g | Protein: 7.1g | Cholesterol: 0mg | Sodium: 501.1mg

INGREDIENTS

- 1 (16 ounce) can black beans
- 1 small onion, chopped
- 1 clove garlic, chopped
- 1 tablespoon chopped fresh cilantro
- 1/4 teaspoon cayenne pepper
- 1/8 teaspoon salt to taste

DIRECTIONS

1. In a medium saucepan, combine beans, onion, and garlic, and bring to a boil. Reduce heat to medium-low. Season with cilantro, cayenne, and salt. Simmer for 5 minutes, and serve.

LENTIL SOUP WITH LEMON
Servings: 4 | Prep: 35m | Cooks: 40m | Total: 1h15m

NUTRITION FACTS

Calories: 351.4 | Carbohydrates: 37.7g | Protein: 14.6g | Cholesterol: 5.6mg | Sodium: 1247.1mg

INGREDIENTS

- 3 tablespoons olive oil
- 1 (32 ounce) carton chicken broth
- 1 large onion, chopped
- 1 cup red lentils
- 2 cloves garlic, minced
- 1 large carrot, diced
- 1 tablespoon tomato paste
- 2 tablespoons lemon juice, or to taste
- 1 teaspoon ground cumin
- 3 tablespoons chopped fresh cilantro
- 1/4 teaspoon kosher salt, or to taste
- 4 teaspoons extra-virgin olive oil for drizzling

- 1/4 teaspoon freshly ground black pepper
- 1 pinch chili powder
- 1/8 teaspoon chili powder, or to taste

DIRECTIONS

1. Heat 3 tablespoons of olive oil in a large pot over medium-high heat. Stir in the onion and garlic, and cook until the onion has turned golden brown, about 5 minutes. Stir in the tomato paste, cumin, kosher salt, black pepper, and 1/8 teaspoon of chili powder. Cook and stir 2 minutes more until the spices are fragrant.
2. Stir in the chicken broth, lentils, and carrot. Bring to a boil over high heat, then reduce the heat to medium-low, cover, and simmer until the lentils are soft, about 30 minutes.
3. Pour half of the soup into a blender, filling the pitcher no more than halfway full. Hold down the lid of the blender with a folded kitchen towel, and carefully start the blender, using a few quick pulses to get the soup moving before leaving it on to puree. Puree in batches until smooth and pour into a clean pot. Alternately, you can use a stick blender and puree the soup right in the cooking pot. Do not puree all of the soup, leave it a little chunky
4. Stir in the lemon juice and cilantro, then season to taste with salt. Drizzle with olive oil and a sprinkle of chili powder to serve.

ANDREA'S PASTA FAGIOLI
Servings: 8 | Prep: 10m | Cooks: 1h30m | Total: 1h40m

NUTRITION FACTS

Calories: 402.8 | Carbohydrates: 68g | Protein: 16.3g | Cholesterol: 2.9mg | Sodium: 1222.7mg

INGREDIENTS

- 3 tablespoons olive oil
- 1 1/2 teaspoons dried oregano
- 1 onion, quartered then halved
- 1 teaspoon salt
- 2 cloves garlic, minced
- 1 (15 ounce) can cannellini beans
- 1 (29 ounce) can tomato sauce
- 1 (15 ounce) can navy beans
- 5 1/2 cups water
- 1/3 cup grated Parmesan cheese
- 1 tablespoon dried parsley
- 1 pound ditalini past

- 1 1/2 teaspoons dried basil

DIRECTIONS

1. In a large pot over medium heat, cook onion in olive oil until translucent. Stir in garlic and cook until tender. Reduce heat, and stir in tomato sauce, water, parsley, basil, oregano, salt, cannelini beans, navy beans and Parmesan. Simmer 1 hour.
2. Bring a large pot of lightly salted water to a boil. Add pasta and cook for 8 to 10 minutes or until al dente; drain. Stir into soup.

LENTILS AND RICE WITH FRIED ONIONS (MUJADARRAH)

Servings: 4 | Prep: 10m | Cooks: 40m | Total: 50m

NUTRITION FACTS

Calories: 534.8 | Carbohydrates: 69.1g | Protein: 17.3g | Cholesterol: 0.9mg | Sodium: 311.9mg

INGREDIENTS

- 6 tablespoons olive oil
- 3/4 cup uncooked long-grain white rice
- 1 large white onion, sliced into rings
- 1/2 teaspoon salt and pepper to taste

- 1 1/3 cups uncooked green lentils
- 1/4 cup plain yogurt or sour cream

DIRECTIONS

1. Heat the olive oil in a large skillet over medium heat. Stir in the onions, and cook about 10 minutes, until browned. Remove from heat, and set aside.
2. Place lentils in a medium saucepan with enough lightly salted water to cover. Bring to a boil, reduce heat, and simmer about 15 minutes.
3. Stir rice and enough water to cover into the saucepan with the lentils. Season with salt and pepper. Cover saucepan, and continue to simmer 15 to 20 minutes, until rice and lentils are tender.
4. Mix half the onions into the lentil mixture. Top with yogurt or sour cream and remaining onions to serve.

SLOW COOKER SPICY BLACK-EYED PEAS

Servings: 10 | Prep: 30m | Cooks: 6h | Total: 6h30m

NUTRITION FACTS

Calories: 199 | Carbohydrates: 30.2g | Fat: 2.9g | Protein: 14.1g | Cholesterol: 10mg | Sodium: 341mg

INGREDIENTS

- 6 cups water
- 1 cube chicken bouillon
- 1 pound dried black-eyed peas, sorted and rinsed
- 1 onion, diced
- 2 cloves garlic, diced
- 1 red bell pepper, stemmed, seeded, and diced
- 1 jalapeno chile, seeded and minced
- 8 ounces diced ham
- 4 slices bacon, chopped
- 1/2 teaspoon cayenne pepper
- 1 1/2 teaspoons cumin
- salt, to taste
- 1 teaspoon ground black pepper

DIRECTIONS

1. Pour the water into a slow cooker, add the bouillon cube, and stir to dissolve. Combine the black-eyed peas, onion, garlic, bell pepper, jalapeno pepper, ham, bacon, cayenne pepper, cumin, salt, and pepper; stir to blend. Cover the slow cooker and cook on Low for 6 to 8 hours until the beans are tender.

CHICKEN AND CORN CHILI
Servings: 6 | Prep: 15m | Cooks: 12h | Total: 12h15m

NUTRITION FACTS

Calories: 187.9 | Carbohydrates: 22.6g | Protein: 20.4g | Cholesterol: 40.6mg | Sodium: 1012.4mg

INGREDIENTS

- 4 skinless, boneless chicken breast halves
- 1 (16 ounce) jar salsa
- 2 teaspoons garlic powder
- 1 teaspoon ground cumin
- 1 teaspoon chili powder
- 1/4 teaspoon salt to taste
- 1/4 teaspoon ground black pepper to taste
- 1 (11 ounce) can Mexican-style corn
- 1 (15 ounce) can pinto beans

DIRECTIONS

1. Place chicken and salsa in the slow cooker the night before you want to eat this chili. Season with garlic powder, cumin, chili powder, salt, and pepper. Cook 6 to 8 hours on Low setting.
2. About 3 to 4 hours before you want to eat, shred the chicken with 2 forks. Return the meat to the pot, and continue cooking.
3. Stir the corn and the pinto beans into the slow cooker. Simmer until ready to serve.

SMOKIN' SCOVILLES TURKEY CHILI
Servings: 8 | Prep: 10m | Cooks: 1h15m | Total: 1h25m

NUTRITION FACTS

Calories: 327.6 | Carbohydrates: 24.8g | Protein: 28.1g | Cholesterol: 83.8mg | Sodium: 1099mg

INGREDIENTS

- 2 tablespoons olive oil
- 1 teaspoon ground black pepper
- 1 onion, chopped
- 1 (1 ounce) envelope instant hot chocolate mix
- 5 cloves garlic, minced

- 2 small green bell peppers, seeded and chopped

- 1 habanero pepper, seeded and chopped

- 2 pounds lean ground turkey

- 2 tablespoons chili powder

- 2 teaspoons red pepper flakes

- 1 tablespoon paprika

- 1 tablespoon ground cumin

- 2 teaspoons seasoned salt

- 1 tablespoon Worcestershire sauce

- 1 teaspoon liquid smoke flavoring

- 2 (14.5 ounce) cans diced tomatoes with green chile peppers, drained

- 1 (8 ounce) can tomato sauce

- 1 (15 ounce) can kidney beans, drained

- 1/2 cup cheap beer

- 1/2 cup canned whole kernel corn

- 2 teaspoons dried oregano
- 1 tablespoon hot pepper sauce

DIRECTIONS

1. Heat the olive oil in a large saucepan over medium heat. Add the onion, garlic, green peppers and habanero pepper; cook and stir until the onion is transparent. Push these to one side of the pot, and crumble in the ground turkey. Cover, and cook for about 5 minutes, stirring occasionally, or until the meat is no longer pink. Stir everything together so the garlic doesn't burn.
2. Season with chili powder, red pepper flakes, paprika, cumin, oregano, pepper, hot cocoa mix and seasoned salt. Stir in Worcestershire sauce, liquid smoke, diced tomatoes with green chilies, tomato sauce and kidney beans. Crack open a beer, and pour in about 1/3. Drink or discard the rest. Partially cover the pan, and simmer over medium heat for about 50 minutes, stirring occasionally.
3. Mix in the corn and hot pepper sauce, and simmer for about 10 more minutes. Remove from the heat and allow to cool for a few minutes before serving.

SPICED SWEET ROASTED RED PEPPER HUMMUS

Servings: 8 | Prep: 15m | Cooks: 1h | Total: 1h15m | Additional: 1h

NUTRITION FACTS

Calories: 64 | Carbohydrates: 9.6g | Fat: 2.2g | Protein: 2.5g | Cholesterol: 0mg | Sodium: 370mg

INGREDIENTS

- 1 (15 ounce) can garbanzo beans, drained

- 1 (4 ounce) jar roasted red peppers

- 3 tablespoons lemon juice

- 1 1/2 tablespoons tahini

- 1 clove garlic, minced

- 1/2 teaspoon ground cumin

- 1/2 teaspoon cayenne pepper

- 1/4 teaspoon salt

- 1 tablespoon chopped fresh parsley

DIRECTIONS

1. In an electric blender or food processor, puree the chickpeas, red peppers, lemon juice, tahini, garlic, cumin, cayenne, and salt. Process, using long pulses, until the mixture is fairly smooth, and slightly fluffy. Make sure to scrape the mixture off the sides of the food processor or blender in between pulses. Transfer to a serving bowl and refrigerate for at least

1 hour. (The hummus can be made up to 3 days ahead and refrigerated. Return to room temperature before serving.)
2. Sprinkle the hummus with the chopped parsley before serving.

JUST LIKE WENDY'S® CHILI

Servings: 10 | Prep: 15m | Cooks: 1h20m | Total: 1h35m

NUTRITION FACTS

Calories: 326.1 | Carbohydrates: 28.8g | Protein: 22.6g | Cholesterol: 55.1mg | Sodium: 1521mg

INGREDIENTS

- 2 tablespoons olive oil
- 2 pounds ground beef
- 2 stalks celery, chopped
- 1 onion, chopped
- 1 (14 ounce) can tomato sauce
- 1 cup water
- 2 (1.25 ounce) packages chili seasoning (such as McCormick® Mild Chili Seasoning Mix)
- 1 (14 ounce) can kidney beans, undrained

- 1 green bell pepper, chopped
- 3 (14 ounce) cans stewed tomatoes
- 1 (10 ounce) can diced tomatoes with green chiles (such as RO*TEL)
- 1 (14 ounce) can pinto beans, undrained
- 1 pinch salt and ground black pepper to taste
- 1 tablespoon white vinegar, or more to taste

DIRECTIONS

1. Heat olive oil in a large pot over medium-high heat. Press ground beef into the hot oil to form one large patty; let the bottom brown, 8 to 10 minutes. Stir and break the ground beef into crumbles and cook until no longer pink, about 5 more minutes.
2. Stir celery, onion, and green bell pepper into ground beef and cook until onion is translucent, about 5 minutes; pour in stewed tomatoes, diced tomatoes with green chiles, tomato sauce, and water. Break apart large chunks of stewed tomatoes. Stir in chili seasoning.
3. Mix kidney beans and pinto beans into chili, season with salt and black pepper, and bring to a boil. Reduce heat to low and simmer for 1 hour. Mix vinegar into chili.

CHICKEN FIESTA SALAD

Servings: 4 | Prep: 10m | Cooks: 30m | Total: 40m

NUTRITION FACTS

Calories: 210.8 | Carbohydrates: 42.2g | Protein: 23g | Cholesterol: 35.9mg | Sodium: 1605.6mg

INGREDIENTS

- 2 skinless, boneless chicken breast halves
- 1 (1.27 ounce) packet dry fajita seasoning, divided
- 1 tablespoon vegetable oil
- 1 (15 ounce) can black beans, rinsed and drained
- 1 (11 ounce) can Mexican-style corn
- ½ cup salsa
- 1 (10 ounce) package mixed salad greens
- 1 onion, chopped
- 1 tomato, cut into wedges

DIRECTIONS

1. Rub chicken evenly with 1/2 the fajita seasoning. Heat the oil in a skillet over medium heat, and cook the chicken 8 minutes on each side, or until juices run clear; set aside.
2. In a large saucepan, mix beans, corn, salsa and other 1/2 of fajita seasoning. Heat over medium heat until warm.
3. Prepare the salad by tossing the greens, onion and tomato. Top salad with chicken and dress with the bean and corn mixture.

CORN AND BLACK BEAN SALAD

Servings: 4 | Prep: 10m | Cooks: 13h20m | Total: 13h30m | Additional: 13h20m

NUTRITION FACTS

Calories: 214.2 | Carbohydrates: 28.6g | Protein: 7.5g | Cholesterol: 0mg | Sodium: 805mg

INGREDIENTS

- 1/4 cup balsamic vinegar
- 2 tablespoons vegetable oil
- 1/2 teaspoon salt
- 1/2 teaspoon white sugar
- 1/2 teaspoon ground black pepper
- 1/2 teaspoon ground cumin
- 1/2 teaspoon chili powder
- 3 tablespoons chopped fresh cilantro
- 1 (15 ounce) can black beans, rinsed and dra
- 1 (8.75 ounce) can sweet corn, drained

DIRECTIONS

1. In a small bowl, mix together balsamic vinegar, oil, salt, sugar, black pepper, cumin, and chili powder.
2. In a medium bowl, stir together black beans and corn. Toss with vinegar and oil dressing, and garnish with cilantro. Cover, and refrigerate overnight.

MOCK TUNA SALAD

Servings: 4 | Prep: 20m | Cooks: 0m | Total: 20m

NUTRITION FACTS

Calories: 219.6 | Carbohydrates: 32.7g | Protein: 7g | Cholesterol: 2.6mg | Sodium: 506.6mg

INGREDIENTS

- 1 (19 ounce) can garbanzo beans (chickpeas), drained and mashed
- 2 tablespoons mayonnaise
- 2 teaspoons spicy brown mustard
- 1 tablespoon sweet pickle relish
- 2 green onions, chopped
- salt and pepper to taste

DIRECTIONS

1. In a medium bowl, combine garbanzo beans, mayonnaise, mustard, relish, chopped green onions, salt and pepper. Mix well.

MAKE AHEAD LUNCH WRAPS
Servings: 16 | Prep: 30m | Cooks: 35m | Total: 1h5m

NUTRITION FACTS

Calories: 557.3 | Carbohydrates: 80.8g | Protein: 22.9g | Cholesterol: 30.4mg | Sodium: 1312.1mg

INGREDIENTS

- 2 cups uncooked brown rice
- 4 cups water
- 4 (15 ounce) cans black beans
- 2 (15.5 ounce) cans pinto beans
- 1 (10 ounce) can whole kernel corn
- 1 (10 ounce) can diced tomatoes and green chiles
- 16 (10 inch) flour tortillas
- 1 pound shredded pepperjack cheese

DIRECTIONS

1. Combine rice and water in a saucepan, and bring to a boil. Reduce heat to low, cover, and simmer for 35 to 40 minutes, or until tender. Remove from heat, and cool.
2. Place black beans and pinto beans into a colander or strainer, and rinse. Add corn and diced tomatoes with green chilies, and toss to mix. Transfer to a large bowl, and mix in rice and cheese.
3. Divide the mixture evenly among the tortillas, and roll up. Wrap individually in plastic wrap, place into a large freezer bag, and freeze. Reheat as needed in the microwave for lunch or snacks.

EXTRA EASY HUMMUS

Servings: 4 | Prep: 5m | Cooks: 0m | Total: 5m

NUTRITION FACTS

Calories: 118.2 | Carbohydrates: 16.5g | Protein: 3.7g | Cholesterol: 0mg | Sodium: 501.9mg

INGREDIENTS

• 1 (15 ounce) can garbanzo beans, drained, liquid reserved	• 1/2 teaspoon salt
• 1 clove garlic, crushed	• 1 tablespoon olive oil

- 2 teaspoons ground cumin

DIRECTIONS

1. In a blender or food processor combine garbanzo beans, garlic, cumin, salt and olive oil. Blend on low speed, gradually adding reserved bean liquid, until desired consistency is achieved.

VEGETARIAN KALE SOUP

Servings: 8 | Prep: 25m | Cooks: 30m | Total: 55m

NUTRITION FACTS

Calories: 277.3 | Carbohydrates: 50.9g | Protein: 9.6g | Cholesterol: 0mg | Sodium: 372.2mg

INGREDIENTS

- 2 tablespoons olive oil
- 1 yellow onion, chopped
- 2 tablespoons chopped garlic
- (15 ounce) can diced tomatoes
- 6 white potatoes, peeled and cubed
- 2 (15 ounce) cans cannellini beans (drained if desired)

- 1 bunch kale, stems removed and leaves chopped

- 8 cups water

- 6 cubes vegetable bouillon (such as Knorr)

- 1 tablespoon Italian seasoning

- 2 tablespoons dried parsley

- 1 pinch salt and pepper to taste

DIRECTIONS

1. Heat the olive oil in a large soup pot; cook the onion and garlic until soft. Stir in the kale and cook until wilted, about 2 minutes. Stir in the water, vegetable bouillon, tomatoes, potatoes, beans, Italian seasoning, and parsley. Simmer soup on medium heat for 25 minutes, or until potatoes are cooked through. Season with salt and pepper to taste.

LENTIL AND SAUSAGE SOUP

Servings: 10 | Prep: 15m | Cooks: 3h | Total: 3h15m

NUTRITION FACTS

Calories: 353 | Carbohydrates: 50.2g | Protein: 18.9g | Cholesterol: 17.3mg | Sodium: 1008.5mg

INGREDIENTS

- 1/2 pound sweet Italian sausage
- 1 large onion, chopped
- 1 stalk celery, finely chopped
- 1 tablespoon chopped garlic
- 1 (16 ounce) package dry lentils, rinsed
- 1 cup shredded carrot
- 1 (28 ounce) can diced tomatoes
- 1 tablespoon garlic powder
- 1 tablespoon chopped fresh parsley
- 2 bay leaves
- 1/2 teaspoon dried oregano
- 1/4 teaspoon dried thyme

- 8 cups water
- 2 (14.5 ounce) cans chicken broth
- 1/4 teaspoon dried basil
- 1 tablespoon salt, or to taste

DIRECTIONS

1. Place sausage in a large pot. Cook over medium high heat until evenly brown. Add onion, celery and chopped garlic, and saute until tender and translucent. Stir in lentils, carrot, water, chicken broth and tomatoes. Season with garlic powder, parsley, bay leaves, oregano, thyme, basil, salt and pepper. Bring to a boil, then reduce heat. Cover, and simmer for 2 1/2 to 3 hours, or until lentils are tender.
2. Stir in pasta, and cook 15 to 20 minutes, or until pasta is tender.

BLACK BEANS AND PORK CHOPS
Servings: 4 | Prep: 5m | Cooks: 25m | Total: 30m

NUTRITION FACTS

Calories: 392 | Carbohydrates:21.8g | Fat: 18.7g | Protein: 33.8g | Cholesterol: 72mg | Sodium: 837mg

INGREDIENTS

- 4 bone-in pork chops

- ground black pepper to taste
- 1 tablespoon olive oil
- 1 (15 ounce) can black beans, with liquid
- 1 cup salsa
- 1 tablespoon chopped fresh cilantro

DIRECTIONS

1. Season pork chops with pepper.
2. Heat oil in a large skillet over medium-high heat. Cook pork chops in hot oil until browned, 3 to 5 minutes per side.
3. Pour beans and salsa over pork chops and season with cilantro. Bring to a boil, reduce heat to medium-low, cover the skillet, and simmer until pork chops are cooked no longer pink in the center, 20 to 35 minutes. An instant-read thermometer inserted into the center should read 145 degrees F (63 degrees C).

TEX-MEX TURKEY SOUP

Servings: 6 | Prep: 10m | Cooks: 40m | Total: 50m

NUTRITION FACTS

Calories: 683 | Carbohydrates: 112.3g | Protein: 59.2g | Cholesterol: 112.3mg | Sodium: 2036.3mg

INGREDIENTS

- 1 tablespoon olive oil

- 1/2 cup minced onion

- 3 cloves garlic, minced

- 2 teaspoons chili powder

- 1/2 teaspoon cumin

- 1/2 teaspoon oregano

- 4 cups water

- 1 (10.75 ounce) can condensed tomato soup

- 1 tablespoon dried parsley

- 3 chicken bouillon cubes

- 1 (14 ounce) can black beans, rinsed, drained

- 2 cups frozen corn

- 1/2 cup sour cream

- 1/4 cup chopped fresh cilantro

- 6 cups corn tortilla chips

- 3/4 cup chopped green onion

- 1 (28 ounce) can diced tomatoes
- 1 cup salsa
- 4 cups shredded cooked turkey
- 1 cup shredded Cheddar-Monterey Jack cheese blend
- 1/2 cup chopped fresh cilantro
- 1/2 cup sour cream

DIRECTIONS

1. Heat olive oil in a large saucepan over medium heat. Add minced onions and cook until onions begin to soften, about 4 minutes. Add garlic, chili powder, cumin and oregano and cook, stirring, for 1 minute.
2. Stir in water, tomato soup, diced tomatoes, salsa, shredded turkey, parsley and bouillon cubes. Bring to a boil, then reduce heat, and simmer 5 minutes or until bouillon cubes dissolve. Add black beans, corn, sour cream and cilantro. Simmer for 20 to 30 minutes.
3. Serve soup with crushed tortilla chips, chopped green onion, shredded cheese and additional cilantro and sour cream.

ITALIAN VEGETABLE SOUP

Servings: 8| Prep: 20m | Cooks: 50m | Total: 1h10m

NUTRITION FACTS

Calories: 440.7 | Carbohydrates: 52.5g | Fat: g | Protein: 22.4g | Cholesterol: 48.4mg | Sodium: 1295mg

INGREDIENTS

- 1 pound ground beef
- 1 cup chopped onion
- 1 cup chopped celery
- 1 cup chopped carrots
- 2 cloves garlic, minced
- 1 (14.5 ounce) can peeled and diced tomatoes
- 1 (15 ounce) can tomato sauce
- 5 teaspoons beef bouillon granules
- 1 tablespoon dried parsley
- ½ teaspoon dried oregano
- ½ teaspoon dried basil
- 2 cups chopped cabbage
- 1 (15.25 ounce) can whole kernel corn
- 1 (15 ounce) can green beans

- 2 (19 ounce) cans kidney beans, drained and rinsed

- 2 cups water

- 1 cup macaroni

DIRECTIONS

1. Place ground beef in a large soup pot. Cook over medium heat until evenly browned. Drain excess fat. Stir in onion, celery, carrots, garlic, chopped tomatoes, tomato sauce, beans, water and bouillon. Season with parsley, oregano and basil. Simmer for 20 minutes
2. Stir in cabbage, corn, green beans and pasta. Bring to a boil, then reduce heat. Simmer until vegetables are tender and pasta is al dente. Add more water if needed.

GREEK PASTA WITH TOMATOES AND WHITE BEANS

Servings: 4 | Prep: 10m | Cooks: 15m | Total: 25m

NUTRITION FACTS

Calories: 459.8 | Carbohydrates: 79g | Protein: 23.4g | Cholesterol: 16.7mg | Sodium: 592.8mg

INGREDIENTS

• (14.5 ounce) cans Italian-style diced tomatoes	• ounces penne pasta
• 1 (19 ounce) can cannellini beans, drained and rinsed	• 1/2 cup crumbled feta cheese

- 10 ounces fresh spinach, washed and chopped

DIRECTIONS

1. Cook the pasta in a large pot of boiling salted water until al dente.
2. Meanwhile, combine tomatoes and beans in a large non-stick skillet. Bring to a boil over medium high heat. Reduce heat, and simmer 10 minutes.
3. Add spinach to the sauce; cook for 2 minutes or until spinach wilts, stirring constantly.
4. Serve sauce over pasta, and sprinkle with feta.

WHITE CHILI I

Servings: 4 | Prep: 10m | Cooks: 25m | Total: 35m

NUTRITION FACTS

Calories: 356.7| Carbohydrates: 27.8g | Protein: 39.3g | Cholesterol: 81.1mg | Sodium: 490.1mg

INGREDIENTS

• ablespoon olive oil	• easpoon dried oregano
• 4 skinless, boneless chicken breast halves	• 1/2 teaspoon dried cilantro

- cubed
- 1 onion, chopped
- 1 1/4 cups chicken broth
- 1 (4 ounce) can diced green chiles
- 1 teaspoon garlic powder
- 1 teaspoon ground cumin
- 1/8 teaspoon cayenne pepper
- 1 (15 ounce) can cannellini beans, drained and rinsed
- 2 green onions, chopped
- 2 ounces shredded Monterey Jack cheese

DIRECTIONS

1. Heat oil in a large saucepan over medium-high heat. Cook chicken and onion in oil 4 to 5 minutes, or until onion is tender.
2. Stir in the chicken broth, green chiles, garlic powder, cumin, oregano, cilantro, and cayenne pepper. Reduce heat, and simmer for 15 minutes.

3. Stir in the beans, and simmer for 5 more minutes, or until chicken is no longer pink and juices run clear. Garnish with green onion and shredded cheese.

GREEK GARBANZO BEAN SALAD
Servings: 8 | Prep: 10m | Cooks: 0m | Total: 2h10m | Additional: 2h

NUTRITION FACTS

Calories: 214 | Carbohydrates: 25.5g | Fat: 11.5g | Protein: 5.2g | Cholesterol: 3mg | Sodium: 1067mg

INGREDIENTS

- 2 (15 ounce) cans garbanzo beans, drained
- 2 cucumbers, halved lengthwise and sliced
- 12 cherry tomatoes, halved
- 1/2 red onion, chopped
- 2 cloves garlic, minced
- 1 ounce crumbled feta cheese
- 1/2 cup Italian-style salad dressing
- 1/2 lemon, juiced
- 1/2 teaspoon garlic salt

- 1/2 teaspoon ground black pepper

- 1 (15 ounce) can black olives, drained and chopped

DIRECTIONS

1. Combine the beans, cucumbers, tomatoes, red onion, garlic, olives, cheese, salad dressing, lemon juice, garlic salt and pepper. Toss together and refrigerate 2 hours before serving. Serve chilled.

MIDDLE EASTERN RICE WITH BLACK BEANS AND CHICKPEAS

Servings: 8 | Prep: 15m | Cooks: 45m | Total: 1h

NUTRITION FACTS

Calories: 452.5 | Carbohydrates: 55.7g | Protein: 30.7g | Cholesterol: 65.4mg | Sodium: 1174.3mg

INGREDIENTS

- 1 tablespoon olive oil
- 1 1/2 pounds ground turkey
- 1 clove garlic, minced
- 2 (15 ounce) cans garbanzo beans

- 1 cup uncooked basmati rice

- 2 teaspoons ground cumin

- 2 teaspoons ground coriander

- 1 teaspoon ground turmeric

- 1 teaspoon ground cayenne pepper

- 1 quart chicken stock

- (chickpeas), drained and rinsed

- 2 (15 ounce) cans black beans, drained and rinsed

- 1 bunch chopped fresh cilantro

- 1 bunch chopped fresh parsley

- 1/4 cup pine nuts

- 1 pinch salt and ground black pepper to taste

DIRECTIONS

1. Heat the olive oil in a large saucepan over medium heat. Stir in garlic, and cook 1 minute. Stir in rice, cumin,

coriander, turmeric, and cayenne pepper. Cook and stir 5 minutes, then pour in chicken stock. Bring to a boil. Reduce heat to low, cover, and simmer 20 minutes.
2. Place the turkey in a skillet over medium heat, and cook until evenly brown.
3. Gently mix cooked turkey, garbanzo beans, black beans, cilantro, parsley, and pine nuts into the cooked rice. Season with salt and pepper.

MOROCCAN LENTIL SOUP
Servings: 6 | Prep: 20m | Cooks: 1h45m | Total: 2h5m

NUTRITION FACTS

Calories: 329 | Carbohydrates: 56.5g | Fat: 3.6g | Protein: 18.3g | Cholesterol: 0mg | Sodium: 317mg

INGREDIENTS

- 2 onions, chopped
- 2 cloves garlic, minced
- 1 teaspoon grated fresh ginger
- 6 cups water
- 1/2 cup diced carrots
- 1/2 cup chopped celery
- 1 teaspoon garam masala
- 1 1/2 teaspoons ground cardamom

- 1 cup red lentils
- 1 (15 ounce) can garbanzo beans, drained
- 1 (19 ounce) can cannellini beans
- 1 (14.5 ounce) can diced tomatoes
- 1/2 teaspoon ground cayenne pepper
- 1/2 teaspoon ground cumin
- 1 tablespoon olive oil

DIRECTIONS

1. In large pot saute; the onions, garlic, and ginger in a little olive oil for about 5 minutes.
2. Add the water, lentils, chick peas, white kidney beans, diced tomatoes, carrots, celery, garam masala, cardamom, cayenne pepper and cumin. Bring to a boil for a few minutes then simmer for 1 to 1 1/2 hours or longer, until the lentils are soft.
3. Puree half the soup in a food processor or blender. Return the pureed soup to the pot, stir and enjoy!

EASY RED BEANS AND RICE
Servings: 8 | Prep: 10m | Cooks: 30m | Total: 40m

NUTRITION FACTS

Calories: 289.1 | Carbohydrates: 42.4g | Protein: 16.3g | Cholesterol: 35mg | Sodium: 807.8mg

INGREDIENTS

- 2 cups water
- 1 cup uncooked rice
- 1 (16 ounce) package turkey kielbasa, cut diagonally into 1/4 inch slices
- 1 onion, chopped
- 1 green bell pepper, chopped
- 1 clove chopped garlic
- 2 (15 ounce) cans canned kidney beans, drained
- 1 (16 ounce) can whole peeled tomatoes, chopped
- 1/2 teaspoon dried oregano
- salt to taste
- 1/2 teaspoon pepper

DIRECTIONS

1. In a saucepan, bring water to a boil. Add rice and stir. Reduce heat, cover and simmer for 20 minutes.
2. In a large skillet over low heat, cook sausage for 5 minutes. Stir in onion, green pepper and garlic; saute until tender. Pour in beans and tomatoes with juice. Season with oregano, salt and pepper. Simmer uncovered for 20 minutes. Serve over rice.

BLACK-EYED PEA GUMBO
Servings: 8 | Prep: 15m | Cooks: 55m | Total: 1h10m

NUTRITION FACTS

Calories: 272.4 | Carbohydrates: 48.5g | Protein: 12.5g | Cholesterol: 0mg | Sodium: 869.7mg

INGREDIENTS

- 1 tablespoon olive oil
- 1 medium onion, chopped
- 1 medium green bell pepper, chopped
- 1 cup brown rice
- 4 (15 ounce) cans black-eyed peas with liquid
- 1 (10 ounce) can diced tomatoes and green chiles

- 5 stalks celery, chopped
- 1 (14.5 ounce) can diced tomatoes
- 2 cups chicken broth
- 2 cloves garlic, finely chopped

DIRECTIONS

1. Heat the olive oil in a large saucepan over medium heat, and cook the onion, pepper, and celery until tender. Pour in the chicken broth, and mix in rice, black-eyed peas with liquid, diced tomatoes and green chiles, diced tomatoes, and garlic. Bring to a boil, reduce heat to low, and simmer 45 minutes, or until rice is tender. Add water if soup is too thick.

VEGETARIAN MEXICAN INSPIRED STUFFED PEPPERS

Servings: 4 | Prep: 15m | Cooks: 40m | Total: 55m

NUTRITION FACTS

Calories: 509 | Carbohydrates: 55.5g | Fat: 22.8g | Protein: 23.8g | Cholesterol: 55mg | Sodium: 3756mg

INGREDIENTS

- 1 tablespoon salt
- 1 (14.5 ounce) can chili-style diced tomatoes

- 4 large green bell peppers - tops, seeds, and membranes removed
- 1 teaspoon chili powder
- 1 tablespoon olive oil
- 1 teaspoon garlic salt
- 1/2 cup chopped onion
- 1/2 teaspoon ground cumin
- 2 cups cooked rice
- 1/2 teaspoon salt
- 1 (15 ounce) can black beans, drained and rinsed
- 1 (8 ounce) package shredded Mexican cheese blend (such as Sargento® Authentic Mexican)

DIRECTIONS

1. Preheat oven to 350 degrees F (175 degrees C).
2. Bring a large pot of water and 1 tablespoon salt to a boil; cook green bell peppers in the boiling water until slightly softened, 3 to 4 minutes. Drain.
3. Heat olive oil in a skillet over medium heat; cook and stir onion in the hot oil until softened and transparent, 5 to 10

minutes.
4. Mix rice, black beans, tomatoes, and cooked onion in a large bowl. Add chili powder, garlic salt, cumin, 1/2 teaspoon salt; stir until evenly mixed. Fold 1 1/2 cups Mexican cheese blend into rice mixture. Spoon rice mixture into each bell pepper; arrange peppers in 9x9-inch baking dish. Sprinkle peppers with remaining Mexican cheese blend.
5. Bake in the preheated oven until cheese is melted and bubbling, about 30 minutes.

PASTA FAGIOLI

Servings: 4 | Prep: 10m | Cooks: 40m | Total: 50m

NUTRITION FACTS

Calories: 224.6 | Carbohydrates: 37.3g | Protein: 11g | Cholesterol: 2.3mg | Sodium: 757.8mg

INGREDIENTS

- 1 tablespoon olive oil
- 2 stalks celery, chopped
- 1 onion, chopped
- 3 cloves garlic, minced
- 2 teaspoons dried parsley
- 1 teaspoon Italian seasoning
- salt to taste
- 1 (14.5 ounce) can chicken broth
- 2 medium tomatoes, peeled and chopped
- 1 (8 ounce) can tomato sauce
- 1/2 cup uncooked spinach pasta
- 1 (15 ounce) can cannellini beans, with liquid

- 1/4 teaspoon crushed red pepper flakes

DIRECTIONS

1. Heat olive oil in a large saucepan over medium heat. Cook celery, onion, garlic, parsley, Italian seasoning, red pepper flakes, and salt in the hot oil until onion is translucent, about 5 minutes. Stir in chicken broth, tomatoes and tomato sauce, and simmer on low for 15 to 20 minutes.
2. Add pasta and cook 10 minutes, until pasta is tender.
3. Add undrained beans and mix well. Heat through. Serve with grated Parmesan cheese sprinkled on top.

BROWN RICE AND BLACK BEAN CASSEROLE

Servings: 8 | Prep: 15m | Cooks: 1h35m | Total: 1h50m

NUTRITION FACTS

Calories: 337.1 | Carbohydrates: 11.5g | Protein: 25.3g | Cholesterol: 76.7mg | Sodium: 363.2mg

INGREDIENTS

- 1/3 cup brown rice
- 1 cup vegetable broth
- 1/2 teaspoon cumin
- 1 pinch salt to taste

- 1 tablespoon olive oil
- 1/3 cup diced onion
- 1 medium zucchini, thinly sliced
- 2 cooked skinless boneless chicken breast halves, chopped
- 1/2 cup sliced mushrooms
- 1 pinch ground cayenne pepper to taste
- 1 (15 ounce) can black beans, drained
- 1 (4 ounce) can diced green chile peppers, drained
- 1/3 cup shredded carrots
- 2 cups shredded Swiss cheese

DIRECTIONS

1. Mix the rice and vegetable broth in a pot, and bring to a boil. Reduce heat to low, cover, and simmer 45 minutes, or until rice is tender.
2. Preheat oven to 350 degrees F (175 degrees C). Lightly grease a large casserole dish.
3. Heat the olive oil in a skillet over medium heat, and cook the onion until tender. Mix in the zucchini, chicken, and

mushrooms. Season with cumin, salt, and ground cayenne pepper. Cook and stir until zucchini is lightly browned and chicken is heated through.
4. In large bowl, mix the cooked rice, onion, zucchini, chicken, mushrooms, beans, chiles, carrots, and 1/2 the Swiss cheese. Transfer to the prepared casserole dish, and sprinkle with remaining cheese.
5. Cover casserole loosely with foil, and bake 30 minutes in the preheated oven. Uncover, and continue baking 10 minutes, or until bubbly and lightly browned.

JERRE'S BLACK BEAN AND PORK TENDERLOIN SLOW COOKER CHILI
Servings: 8 | Prep: 10m | Cooks: 10h | Total: 10h10m

NUTRITION FACTS

Calories: 245 | Carbohydrates: 31.9g | Fat: 2.8g | Protein: 24g | Cholesterol: 37mg | Sodium: 1045mg

INGREDIENTS

- 1 1/2 pounds pork tenderloin, cut into 2 inch strips
- 1 small onion, coarsely chopped
- 1/2 cup chicken broth
- 1 teaspoon dried oregano

- 1 small red bell pepper, coarsely chopped
- 1 teaspoon ground cumin
- 3 (15 ounce) cans black beans
- 2 teaspoons chili powder
- 1 (16 ounce) jar salsa

DIRECTIONS

1. Combine pork tenderloin, onion, red pepper, black beans, salsa, chicken broth, oregano, cumin, and chili powder in a slow cooker. Set to Low and cook for 8 to 10 hours.
2. Break up pieces of cooked pork to thicken the chili before serving.

ROASTED CHICKPEAS

Servings: 4 | Prep: 5m | Cooks: 40m | Total: 45m

NUTRITION FACTS

Calories: 161.3 | Carbohydrates: 19.7g | Protein: 4.2g | Cholesterol: 0mg | Sodium: 337.3mg

INGREDIENTS

- 1 (12 ounce) can chickpeas (garbanzo beans), drained
- 1 pinch garlic salt

- 2 tablespoons olive oil
- 1 pinch cayenne pepper
- 1 pinch salt

DIRECTIONS

1. Preheat oven to 450 degrees F (230 degrees C).
2. Blot chickpeas with a paper towel to dry them. In a bowl, toss chickpeas with olive oil, and season to taste with salt, garlic salt, and cayenne pepper, if using. Spread on a baking sheet, and bake for 30 to 40 minutes, until browned and crunchy. Watch carefully the last few minutes to avoid burning.

AWARD WINNING CHILI

Servings: 8 | Prep: 30m | Cooks: 1h | Total: 1h30m

NUTRITION FACTS

Calories: 373 | Carbohydrates: 22.5g | Protein: 21.7g | Cholesterol: 64.2mg | Sodium: 1168.9mg

INGREDIENTS

- 1 (14.5 ounce) can stewed tomatoes, chopped
- 1/3 cup bottled steak sauce

- 1 (6 ounce) can tomato paste

- 1 carrot, sliced

- 1 onion, chopped

- 2 stalks celery, chopped

- 1/4 cup white wine

- 1 pinch crushed red pepper flakes

- 1/4 cup chopped green bell pepper

- 5 slices bacon

- 1 1/2 pounds ground beef

- 1 (1.25 ounce) package chili seasoning mix

- 1 teaspoon ground cumin

- 1 (15 ounce) can kidney beans, drained

- 1 tablespoon chopped fresh cilantro

DIRECTIONS

1. In a large pot over medium-low heat, combine tomatoes, tomato paste, carrot, onion, celery, wine, pepper flakes, bell peppers and steak sauce.
2. While tomato mixture is simmering, in a large skillet over medium heat, cook bacon until crisp. Remove to paper towels. Cook beef in bacon drippings until brown; drain. Stir chili seasoning into ground beef.
3. Stir seasoned beef, cumin and bacon into tomato mixture. Continue to simmer until vegetables are tender and flavors are well blended.
4. Stir in beans, cilantro and parsley. Heat through and serve.

EASY WHITE CHILI

Servings: 8 | Prep: 15m | Cooks: 30m | Total: 45m

NUTRITION FACTS

Calories: 520.7 | Carbohydrates: 59.2g | Protein: 41.1g | Cholesterol: 53.8mg | Sodium: 935mg

INGREDIENTS

- 2 tablespoons olive oil
- 2 onions, chopped
- 4 cloves garlic, minced
- 2 teaspoons ground cumin
- 2 teaspoons dried oregano
- 1 1/2 teaspoons cayenne pepper

- 4 cooked, boneless chicken breast half, chopped

- 3 (14.5 ounce) cans chicken broth

- 2 (4 ounce) cans canned green chile peppers, chopped

- 5 (14.5 ounce) cans great Northern beans, undrained

- 1 cup shredded Monterey Jack cheese

DIRECTIONS

1. Heat the oil in a large pot over medium heat. Add the onions and garlic and saute for 10 minutes, or until onions are tender. Add the chicken, chicken broth, green chile peppers, cumin, oregano and cayenne pepper and bring to a boil.
2. Reduce heat to low and add the beans. Simmer for 20 to 30 minutes, or until heated thoroughly. Pour into individual bowls and top with the cheese.

BRAZILIAN BLACK BEAN STEW

Servings: 6 | Prep: 15m | Cooks: 30m | Total: 45m

NUTRITION FACTS

Calories: 507.9 | Carbohydrates: 70.7g | Protein: 22.8g | Cholesterol: 30.8mg | Sodium: 1537.7mg

INGREDIENTS

- 1 tablespoon canola oil
- 1/4 pound chorizo sausage, chopped
- 1/3 pound cooked ham, chopped
- 1 medium onion, chopped
- 2 cloves garlic, minced
- 2 (1 pound) sweet potatoes, peeled and diced
- 1 large red bell pepper, diced
- 2 (14.5 ounce) cans diced tomatoes with juice
- 1 small hot green chile pepper, diced
- 1 1/2 cups water
- 2 (16 ounce) cans black beans, rinsed and drained
- 1 mango - peeled, seeded and diced
- 1/4 cup chopped fresh cilantro
- 1/4 teaspoon salt

DIRECTIONS

1. Heat the oil in a large pot over medium heat, and cook the chorizo and ham 2 to 3 minutes. Place the onion in the pot, and cook until tender. Stir in garlic, and cook until tender, then mix in the sweet potatoes, bell pepper, tomatoes with juice, chile pepper, and water. Bring to a boil, reduce heat to low, cover, and simmer 15 minutes, until sweet potatoes are tender.
2. Stir the beans into the pot, and cook uncovered until heated through. Mix in the mango and cilantro, and season with salt.

"PANTRY RAID" CHICKEN ENCHILADA CASSEROLE

Servings: 6 | Prep: 15m | Cooks: 45m | Total: 1h

NUTRITION FACTS

Calories: 487 | Carbohydrates: 45.9g | Protein: 31.2g | Cholesterol: 108.3mg | Sodium: 1911.9mg

INGREDIENTS

- 1 (15 ounce) can tomato sauce
- 1 (15 ounce) can black beans, drained
- 1/4 cup water
- 1/4 cup cream cheese

- 1 envelope taco seasoning mix
- 1 1/2 tablespoons chili powder
- 1 tablespoon vegetable oil
- 1 pound chicken breast tenderloins
- 1 cup shredded Mexican-style cheese blend, or more to taste
- 1 (7.5 ounce) package corn bread mix
- 1 egg
- 1/3 cup milk

DIRECTIONS

1. Preheat the oven to 375 degrees F (190 degrees C). Grease a 9x9-inch baking dish
2. Mix tomato sauce, water, taco seasoning mix, and chili powder together in a saucepan; bring to a simmer over medium heat.
3. Heat vegetable oil in a skillet over medium heat and brown chicken tenderloins on both sides, about 5 minutes per side. Pour tomato sauce mixture over the chicken, bring to a simmer, and cook over medium-low heat until chicken tenderloins are no longer pink inside, about 8 minutes. Transfer chicken to a bowl and shred; return shredded chicken to the sauce. Mix in black beans and cream cheese until thoroughly combined.

4. Pour chicken mixture into prepared baking dish. Top with shredded Mexican cheese. Whisk corn bread mix, egg, and milk in a bowl, and spoon the batter over the chicken mix.
5. Bake in the preheated oven until the casserole is bubbling and the corn bread topping is browned and set, about 30 minutes.

HAM BONE SOUP

Servings: 4 | Prep: 30m | Cooks: 6h | Total: 6h30m

NUTRITION FACTS

Calories: 265.5 | Carbohydrates: 53.3g | Protein: 11.4g | Cholesterol: 0.9mg | Sodium: 2136mg

INGREDIENTS

- 1 ham bone with some meat
- 1 onion, diced
- 1 (14.5 ounce) can peeled and diced tomatoes with juice
- 3 medium (2-1/4" to 3" dia, raw)s potatoes, cubed
- 1 green bell pepper, seeded and cubed
- 4 cups water

- 1 (15.25 ounce) can kidney beans
- 6 cubes chicken bouillon

DIRECTIONS

1. Place the ham bone, onion, tomatoes, kidney beans, potatoes, and green pepper into a 3 quart or larger slow cooker. Dissolve the bouillon cubes in water, and pour into the slow cooker.
2. Cover, and cook on High until warm. Reduce heat to Low, and continue to cook for 5 to 6 hours.

WHITE CHILI

Servings: 8 | Prep: 15m | Cooks: 30m | Total: 45m

NUTRITION FACTS

Calories: 389.6 | Carbohydrates: 28.4g | Protein: 28.8g | Cholesterol: 87.7mg | Sodium: 490.5mg

INGREDIENTS

- 1 pound ground turkey, browned
- 1 cup water
- 1 cup medium salsa
- 2 (14 ounce) cans great Northern beans, rinsed and drained

- 1 cup frozen corn kernels
- 12 ounces pepper jack cheese, cubed

DIRECTIONS

1. In a large pot or saucepan, combine the browned turkey, salsa, corn, water, beans and cheese. Stir together and simmer over low heat for about 30 minutes, or until cheese has melted and chili is hot.

PUMPKIN BLACK BEAN SOUP

Servings: 9 | Prep: 15m | Cooks: 30m | Total: 45m

NUTRITION FACTS

Calories: 150.9 | Carbohydrates: 7.4g | Protein: 7.4g | Cholesterol: 27.7mg | Sodium: 1051.6mg

INGREDIENTS

- 3 (15 ounce) cans black beans, rinsed and drained
- 1/2 teaspoon ground black pepper
- 1 (16 ounce) can diced tomatoes
- 4 cups beef broth
- 1/4 cup butter
- 1 (15 ounce) can pumpkin puree

- 1 1/4 cups chopped onion
- 4 cloves garlic, chopped
- 1 teaspoon salt
- 1/2 pound cubed cooked ham
- 3 tablespoons sherry vinegar

DIRECTIONS

1. Pour 2 cans of the black beans into a food processor or blender, along with the can of tomatoes. Puree until smooth. Set aside.
2. Melt butter in a soup pot over medium heat. Add the onion and garlic, and season with salt and pepper. Cook and stir until the onion is softened. Stir in the bean puree, remaining can of beans, beef broth, pumpkin puree, and sherry vinegar. Mix until well blended, then simmer for about 25 minutes, or until thick enough to coat the back of a metal spoon. Stir in the ham, and heat through before serving.

BLACK BEAN SALAD

Servings: 12 | Prep: 20m | Cooks: 0m | Total: 20m

NUTRITION FACTS

Calories: 159 | Carbohydrates: 24.2g | Protein: 5g | Cholesterol: 0mg | Sodium: 561.9mg

INGREDIENTS

- 1 (15 ounce) can black beans, rinsed and drained
- 2 (15 ounce) cans whole kernel corn, drained
- 8 green onions, chopped
- 2 jalapeno peppers, seeded and minced
- 1 green bell pepper, chopped
- 1 avocado - peeled, pitted, and diced
- 1 (4 ounce) jar pimentos
- 3 eaches tomatoes, seeded and chopped
- 1 cup chopped fresh cilantro
- 1 lime, juiced
- 1/2 cup Italian salad dressing
- 1/2 teaspoon garlic salt

DIRECTIONS

1. In a large bowl, combine the black beans, corn, green onions, jalapeno peppers, bell pepper, avocado, pimentos, tomatoes, cilantro, lime juice, and Italian dressing. Season with garlic salt. Toss, and chill until serving.

SPINACH AND LEEK WHITE BEAN SOUP

Servings: 8 | Prep: 10m | Cooks: 15m | Total: 25m

NUTRITION FACTS

Calories: 179 | Carbohydrates: 30.6g | Fat: 2g | Protein: 9.4g | Cholesterol: 0mg | Sodium: 432mg

INGREDIENTS

- 2 teaspoons olive oil
- 4 leeks, bulb only, chopped
- 2 cloves garlic, chopped
- 2 (16 ounce) cans fat-free chicken broth
- 2 (16 ounce) cans cannellini beans, rinsed and drained
- 2 bay leaves
- 2 teaspoons ground cumin
- 1/2 cup whole wheat couscous
- 2 cups packed fresh spinach
- salt and pepper to taste

DIRECTIONS

1. Heat olive oil in a large saucepan or soup pot over medium heat. Add the leeks and garlic; saute until tender, about 5 minutes. Stir in the chicken broth, cannellini beans, bay leaves and cumin. Bring to a boil, then reduce the heat to low, and stir in the couscous. Cover, and simmer for 5 minutes. Stir in spinach and season with salt and pepper. Serve immediately.

THE ULTIMATE CHILI
Servings: 6 | Prep: 10m | Cooks: 6h10m | Total: 6h20m

NUTRITION FACTS

Calories: 413.7 | Carbohydrates: 49.5g | Protein: 28.4g | Cholesterol: 49.6mg | Sodium: 1015mg

INGREDIENTS

- 1 pound lean ground beef
- salt and pepper to taste
- 3 (15 ounce) cans dark red kidney beans
- 2 tablespoons chili powder
- 1 teaspoon ground cumin
- 1 teaspoon dried parsley

- 3 (14.5 ounce) cans Mexican-style stewed tomatoes
- 2 stalks celery, chopped
- 1 red bell pepper, chopped
- 1/4 cup red wine vinegar
- 1 teaspoon dried basil
- 1 dash Worcestershire sauce
- 1/2 cup red wine

DIRECTIONS

1. In a large skillet over medium-high heat, cook ground beef until evenly browned. Drain off grease, and season to taste with salt and pepper.
2. In a slow cooker, combine the cooked beef, kidney beans, tomatoes, celery, red bell pepper, and red wine vinegar. Season with chili powder, cumin, parsley, basil and Worcestershire sauce. Stir to distribute ingredients evenly.
3. Cook on High for 6 hours, or on Low for 8 hours. Pour in the wine during the last 2 hours.

HEATHER'S CILANTRO, BLACK BEAN, AND CORN SALSA

Servings: 72 | Prep: 25m | Cooks: 0m | Total: 25m

NUTRITION FACTS

Calories: 30 | Carbohydrates: 4.9g | Protein: 1.1g | Cholesterol: 0mg | Sodium: 84.9mg

INGREDIENTS

- 1 (15 ounce) can yellow corn, drained
- 1 (15 ounce) can white corn, drained
- 2 (15 ounce) cans black beans, drained and rinsed
- 1 (14.5 ounce) can Italian-style diced tomatoes, drained
- 1 bunch finely chopped cilantro
- 1 small red onion, finely chopped
- 1 red bell pepper, seeded and chopped
- 1 tablespoon minced garlic
- 1/4 cup lime juice
- 1 avocado - peeled, pitted, and diced

- 5 eaches green onions, finely sliced
- 2 tablespoons olive oil, or to taste

DIRECTIONS

1. Stir the yellow and white corn, black beans, tomatoes, cilantro, green onion, red onion, bell pepper, and garlic in a large bowl. Gently mix in the lime juice and avocado. Drizzle with olive oil to serve.

BUTTER BEAN BURGERS

Servings: 4 | Prep: 15m | Cooks: 10m | Total: 25m

NUTRITION FACTS

Calories: 296.9 | Carbohydrates: 18.5g | Protein: 10.7g | Cholesterol: 61.3mg | Sodium: 565mg

INGREDIENTS

- 1 (15 ounce) can butter beans, drained
- 1/2 cup shredded Cheddar cheese
- 1 small onion, chopped
- 1/4 teaspoon garlic powder
- 1 tablespoon finely chopped jalapeno pepper
- 1 pinch salt and pepper to taste

- 6 saltine crackers, crushed
- 1/4 cup vegetable oil
- 1 egg, beaten

DIRECTIONS

1. In a medium bowl, mash butter beans. Mix in onion, jalapeno pepper, crushed crackers, egg, cheese, garlic powder, salt, and pepper. Divide into 4 equal parts, and shape into patties.
2. Heat oil in a large skillet over medium-high heat; use more or less oil to reach 1/4 inch in depth. Fry patties until golden, about 5 minutes on each side.

QUINOA AND BLACK BEAN CHILI
Servings: 10 | Prep: 30m | Cooks: 30m | Total: 1h

NUTRITION FACTS

Calories: 233 | Carbohydrates: 42g | Fat: 3.5g | Protein: 11.5g | Cholesterol: 0mg | Sodium: 540mg

INGREDIENTS

- 1 cup uncooked quinoa, rinsed
- 1 green bell pepper, chopped
- 2 cups water
- 1 red bell pepper, chopped

- 1 tablespoon vegetable oil
- 1 onion, chopped
- 4 cloves garlic, chopped
- 1 tablespoon chili powder
- 1 tablespoon ground cumin
- 1 (28 ounce) can crushed tomatoes
- 2 (19 ounce) cans black beans, rinsed and drained
- 1 zucchini, chopped
- 1 jalapeno pepper, seeded and minced
- 1 tablespoon minced chipotle peppers in adobo sauce
- 1 teaspoon dried oregano
- salt and ground black pepper to taste
- 1 cup frozen corn
- 1/4 cup chopped fresh cilantro

DIRECTIONS

1. Bring the quinoa and water to a boil in a saucepan over high heat. Reduce heat to medium-low, cover, and simmer until the quinoa is tender, and the water has been absorbed, about 15 to 20 minutes; set aside.
2. Meanwhile, heat the vegetable oil in a large pot over medium heat. Stir in the onion, and cook until the onion softens and turns translucent, about 5 minutes. Add the garlic, chili powder, and cumin; cook and stir 1 minute to release the flavors. Stir in the tomatoes, black beans, green bell pepper, red bell pepper, zucchini, jalapeno pepper, chipotle pepper, and oregano. Season to taste with salt and pepper. Bring to a simmer over high heat, then reduce heat to medium-low, cover, and simmer 20 minutes.
3. After 20 minutes, stir in the reserved quinoa and corn. Cook to reheat the corn for 5 minutes. Remove from the heat, and stir in the cilantro to serve.

HAM AND BEANS

Servings: 7 | Prep: 15m | Cooks: 2h | Total: 10h15m | Additional: 8h

NUTRITION FACTS

Calories: 300.3 | Carbohydrates: 42.8g | Protein: 18.6g | Cholesterol: 18.2mg | Sodium: 423.5mg

INGREDIENTS

- 1 pound dry great Northern beans
- salt and pepper to taste

- 1/2 pound cooked ham, diced
- 1 small onion, diced
- 1/2 cup brown sugar
- 1/4 teaspoon cayenne pepper
- 1 tablespoon dried parsley

DIRECTIONS

1. Rinse beans in a large pot; discard shriveled beans and any small stones. Add 8 cups of cold water. Let stand overnight or at least 8 hours. Drain and rinse beans.
2. Return beans to pot and add ham, onion, brown sugar, salt, pepper, cayenne and parsley and water to cover. Bring to a boil; reduce heat and simmer 1 1/2 to 2 hours, until beans are tender. Add more water if necessary during cooking time.

VEGAN SPLIT PEA SOUP

Servings: 10 | Prep: 10m | Cooks: 3h | Total: 3h10m

NUTRITION FACTS

Calories: 246.6 | Carbohydrates: 45.8g | Protein: 12.7g | Cholesterol: 0mg | Sodium: 386.6mg

INGREDIENTS

- 1 tablespoon vegetable oil
- 1 onion, chopped
- 1 bay leaf
- 3 cloves garlic, minced
- 2 cups dried split peas
- 1/2 cup barley
- 1 1/2 teaspoons salt
- 7 1/2 cups water
- 3 carrots, chopped
- 3 stalks celery, chopped
- 3 medium (2-1/4" to 3" dia, raw)s potatoes, diced
- 1/2 cup chopped parsley
- 1/2 teaspoon dried basil
- 1/2 teaspoon dried thyme
- 1/2 teaspoon ground black pepper

DIRECTIONS

1. In a large pot over medium high heat, saute the oil, onion, bay leaf and garlic for 5 minutes, or until onions are translucent. Add the peas, barley, salt and water. Bring to a boil and reduce heat to low. Simmer for 2 hours, stirring occasionally.
2. Add the carrots, celery, potatoes, parsley, basil, thyme and ground black pepper. Simmer for another hour, or until the peas and vegetables are tender.

NAVY BEAN SOUP

Servings: 9 | Prep: 15m | Cooks: 4h10m | Total: 4h25m

NUTRITION FACTS

Calories: 235.5 | Carbohydrates: 35.7g | Protein: 16.1g | Cholesterol: 14.9mg | Sodium: 878.6mg

INGREDIENTS

- 1 (16 ounce) package dried navy beans
- 6 cups water
- 1 (14.5 ounce) can diced tomatoes
- 2 tablespoons Worcestershire sauce
- 1 tablespoon dried parsley
- 2 teaspoons garlic powder

- 1 onion, chopped
- 2 stalks celery, chopped
- 1 clove garlic, minced
- 1/2 pound chopped ham
- 1 cube chicken bouillon
- 1 bay leaf
- 1 teaspoon salt
- 1/2 teaspoon ground black pepper
- 3 cups water

DIRECTIONS

1. Combine beans, water, tomatoes, onion, celery, garlic, ham, bouillon, Worcestershire sauce, parsley, garlic, and bay leaf in a stock pot; bring to a boil. Lower heat, cover, and simmer for two hours.
2. Add additional water. Season with salt and pepper. Simmer for an additional two hours. Discard bay leaf.

LENTILS AND SPINACH

Servings: 4 | Prep: 10m | Cooks: 55m | Total: 1h5m

NUTRITION FACTS

Calories: 165.3 | Carbohydrates: 24g | Protein: 9.7g | Cholesterol: 0mg | Sodium: 639.1mg

INGREDIENTS

- 1 tablespoon vegetable oil
- 2 white onions, halved and sliced into 1/2 rings
- 3 cloves garlic, minced
- 1/2 cup lentils
- 2 cups water
- 1 (10 ounce) package frozen spinach
- 1 teaspoon salt
- 1 teaspoon ground cumin
- freshly ground black pepper to taste
- 2 cloves garlic, crushed

DIRECTIONS

1. Heat oil in a heavy pan over medium heat. Saute onion for 10 minutes or so, until it begins to turn golden. Add minced garlic and saute for another minute or so.

2. Add lentils and water to the saucepan. Bring mixture to a boil. Cover, lower heat, and simmer about 35 minutes, until lentils are soft (this may take less time, depending on your water and the lentils).
3. Meanwhile cook the spinach in microwave according to package directions. Add spinach, salt and cumin to the saucepan. Cover and simmer until all is heated, about ten minutes. Grind in plenty of pepper and press in extra garlic to taste.

SWEET POTATO AND BLACK BEAN CHILI

Servings: 4 | Prep: 20m | Cooks: 1h10m | Total: 1h30m

NUTRITION FACTS

Calories: 600 | Carbohydrates: 101.4g | Fat: 14.7g | Protein: 20.7g | Cholesterol: 13mg

Sodium: 2119mg

INGREDIENTS

- 2 pounds orange-fleshed sweet potatoes, peeled and cut into cubes

- 1 (28 ounce) can diced tomatoes

- 1/2 teaspoon ground dried chipotle pepper

- 1 cup water, or more as needed

- 1/2 teaspoon salt

- 2 tablespoons olive oil, divided

- 1 onion, diced

- 4 cloves garlic, minced

- 1 red bell pepper, diced

- 1 jalapeno pepper, sliced

- 2 tablespoons ancho chile powder, or to taste

- 1 tablespoon ground cumin

- 1 tablespoon cornmeal

- 1 teaspoon salt, or to taste

- 1 teaspoon white sugar

- 1 teaspoon unsweetened cocoa powder

- 2 (15 ounce) cans black beans, rinsed and drained

- 1 pinch cayenne pepper, or to taste

- 1/2 cup sour cream, for garnish (optional)

- 1/4 cup chopped fresh cilantro, for garnish (optional)

- 1/4 teaspoon dried oregano

DIRECTIONS

1. Preheat oven to 400 degrees F (200 degrees C). Line a baking sheet with parchment paper or a silicone baking mat.
2. Combine sweet potatoes, chipotle pepper, 1/2 teaspoon salt, and 1 tablespoon olive oil in a large bowl and toss to coat. Spread sweet potatoes on the prepared baking sheet in a single layer.
3. Roast sweet potatoes in the preheated oven until the outside is crunchy and inside is tender, 20 to 25 minutes. Allow to cool to room temperature.
4. Cook and stir remaining 1 tablespoon olive oil, onion, garlic, red bell pepper, jalapeno pepper, ancho chile powder, cumin, and dried oregano together in a large pot or Dutch oven over medium heat. Cook and stir until onion is softened, about 5 minutes.
5. Pour tomatoes and water into the onion mixture and bring to a simmer. Add cornmeal, 1 teaspoon salt, sugar, and cocoa powder. Bring to a simmer, stirring constantly, reduce heat to low and simmer for 30 minutes.
6. Stir black beans and cooled sweet potatoes into the onion-tomato mixture. Add more water if mixture is too thick. Simmer until heated through, about 15 minutes. Season with salt and cayenne pepper to taste. Serve topped with sour cream and cilantro.

BEAN QUESADILLAS

Servings: 12 | Prep: 15m | Cooks: 30m | Total: 45m

NUTRITION FACTS

Calories: 504.4 | Carbohydrates: 69.7g | Protein: 14.7g | Cholesterol: 9.9mg | Sodium: 912.6mg

INGREDIENTS

- 1 tablespoon vegetable oil
- 1 onion, finely diced
- 2 cloves garlic, minced
- 1 (15 ounce) can black beans, rinsed and drained
- 1 green bell pepper, chopped
- 2 eaches tomatoes, chopped
- 1/2 (10 ounce) package frozen corn
- 12 (12-inch) flour tortillas
- 1 cup shredded Cheddar cheese
- 1/4 cup vegetable oil

DIRECTIONS

1. Heat 1 tablespoon oil in a skillet over medium heat, and saute the onion and garlic until soft. Mix in beans, bell pepper, tomatoes, and corn; cook until heated through.
2. Spread 6 tortillas with equal amounts of the bean and vegetable mixture. Sprinkle with equal amounts of the Cheddar cheese, and top with the remaining tortillas to form quesadillas.
3. Heat 1/4 cup oil in a large skillet over medium-high heat. Place quesadillas in the skillet and cook, turning once, until cheese is melted and both sides are lightly browned.

TERRY'S TEXAS PINTO BEANS

Servings: 8 | Prep: 15m | Cooks: 2h | Total: 2h15m

NUTRITION FACTS

Calories: 210 | Carbohydrates: 37.9g | Fat: 1.1g | Protein: 13.2g | Cholesterol: 1mg | Sodium: 95mg

INGREDIENTS

- 1 pound dry pinto beans
- 1 (29 ounce) can reduced sodium chicken broth
- 1 large onion, chopped
- 1 fresh jalapeno pepper, chopped
- 2 cloves garlic, minced
- 1/2 cup green salsa
- 1 teaspoon cumin
- 1/2 teaspoon ground black pepper
- water, if needed

DIRECTIONS

1. Place the pinto beans in a large pot, and pour in the chicken broth. Stir in onion, jalapeno, garlic, salsa, cumin, and pepper. Bring to a boil, reduce heat to medium-low, and continue cooking 2 hours, stirring often, until beans are tender. Add water as needed to keep the beans moist.

ESPINACAS CON GARBANZOS (SPINACH WITH GARBANZO BEANS)

Servings: 4 | Prep: 15m | Cooks: 10m | Total: 25m

NUTRITION FACTS

Calories: 169 | Carbohydrates: 26g | Fat: 4.9g | Protein: 7.3g | Cholesterol: 0mg | Sodium: 600mg

INGREDIENTS

- 1 tablespoon extra-virgin olive oil
- 4 cloves garlic, minced
- 1/2 onion, diced
- 1 (10 ounce) box frozen chopped spinach, thawed and drained well
- 1 (12 ounce) can garbanzo beans, drained
- 1/2 teaspoon cumin
- 1/2 teaspoon salt

DIRECTIONS

1. Heat the olive oil in a skillet over medium-low heat. Cook the garlic and onion in the oil until translucent, about 5 minutes. Stir in the spinach, garbanzo beans, cumin, and salt. Use your stirring spoon to lightly mash the beans as the mixture cooks. Allow to cook until thoroughly heated.

PASTA E FAGIOLI A LA CHEZ IVANO
Servings: 20 | Prep: 1h | Cooks: 2h | Total: 3h

NUTRITION FACTS

Calories: 322.4 | Carbohydrates: 27.1g | Protein: 20.6g | Cholesterol: 44.6mg | Sodium: 782.9mg

INGREDIENTS

- 3 pounds lean ground beef
- 1/2 cup olive oil
- 4 cups chopped onion
- 2 cups chopped celery
- 1 (6 ounce) can tomato paste
- 2 1/2 teaspoons dried thyme
- 2 1/2 teaspoons dried basil
- 2 1/2 teaspoons dried oregano

- 2 (4.5 ounce) jars bottled minced garlic
- 1 teaspoon coarsely ground black pepper
- 8 (14 ounce) cans beef broth
- 1 (28 ounce) can crushed tomatoes
- 2 tablespoons dried parsley
- 2 cups ditalini pasta
- 2 (15 ounce) cans kidney beans, drained and rinsed

DIRECTIONS

1. In a large pot over medium heat, cook beef until no longer pink. Drain and set aside.
2. In the same pot, heat the olive oil. Cook onion, celery, garlic and black pepper until vegetables are tender, 10 minutes. Stir in beef broth, crushed tomatoes and tomato paste. Season with thyme, basil, oregano and parsley. Cover, reduce heat and simmer 1 hour. (At this point, you may put the pot on a back burner to keep warm and continue with the next steps about 1 hour prior to serving, if you wish.)
3. Stir in the beef and simmer 15 minutes. Stir in the pasta and cook until al dente, 8 to 10 minutes. Stir in the beans and heat through, 10 to 15 minutes.

VEGAN BEAN TACO FILLING

Servings: 8 | Prep: 15m | Cooks: 15m | Total: 30m

NUTRITION FACTS

Calories: 141.8 | Carbohydrates: 24g | Protein: 7.5g | Cholesterol: 0mg | Sodium: 596.3mg

INGREDIENTS

- 1 tablespoon olive oil
- 1 1//2 tablespoons cumin
- 1 onion, diced
- 1 teaspoon paprika
- 2 cloves garlic, minced
- 1 teaspoon cayenne pepper
- 1 bell pepper, chopped
- 1 teaspoon chili powder
- 2 (14.5 ounce) cans black beans, rinsed, drained, and mashed
- 1 cup salsa
- 2 tablespoons yellow cornmeal

DIRECTIONS

1. Heat olive oil in a medium skillet over medium heat. Stir in onion, garlic, and bell pepper; cook until tender. Stir in mashed beans. Add the cornmeal. Mix in cumin, paprika, cayenne, chili powder, and salsa. Cover, and cook 5 minutes.

ONE SKILLET MEXICAN QUINOA

Servings: 4 | Prep: 15m | Cooks: 25m | Total: 40m

NUTRITION FACTS

Calories: 450.1 | Carbohydrates: 67.1g | Protein: 16.5g | Cholesterol: 1.5mg | Sodium: 1098mg

INGREDIENTS

- 1 tablespoon olive oil
- 1 jalapeno pepper, chopped
- 2 cloves garlic, chopped
- 1 (15 ounce) can black beans, rinsed and
- 1 tablespoon red pepper flakes, or to taste
- 1 1/2 teaspoons chili powder
- 1/2 teaspoon cumin
- 1 pinch kosher salt and ground black

- drained

- 1 (14.5 ounce) can fire-roasted diced tomatoes

- 1 cup yellow corn

- 1 cup quinoa

- 1 cup chicken broth

- pepper to taste

- 1 avocado - peeled, pitted, and diced

- 1 lime, juiced

- 2 tablespoons chopped fresh cilantro

DIRECTIONS

1. Heat oil in a large skillet over medium-high heat. Saute jalapeno pepper and garlic in hot oil until fragrant, about 1 minute.
2. Stir black beans, tomatoes, yellow corn, quinoa, and chicken broth into skillet; season with red pepper flakes, chili powder, cumin, salt, and black pepper. Bring to a boil, cover the skillet with a lid, reduce heat to low, and simmer until quinoa is tender and liquid is mostly absorbed, about 20 minutes. Stir avocado, lime juice, and cilantro into quinoa until combined.

VEGAN RED LENTIL SOUP

Servings: 4 | Prep: 15m | Cooks: 40m | Total: 55m

NUTRITION FACTS

Calories: 303 | Carbohydrates: 34.2g | Fat: 14.6g | Protein: 13g | Cholesterol: 0mg | Sodium: 81mg

INGREDIENTS

- 1 tablespoon peanut oil
- 1 small onion, chopped
- 1 tablespoon minced fresh ginger root
- 1 clove garlic, chopped
- 1 pinch fenugreek seeds
- 1 cup dry red lentils
- 2 cups water
- 1/2 (14 ounce) can coconut milk
- 2 tablespoons tomato paste
- 1 teaspoon curry powder
- 1 pinch cayenne pepper
- 1 pinch ground nutmeg

- 1 cup butternut squash - peeled, seeded, and cubed
- salt and pepper to taste
- 1/3 cup finely chopped fresh cilantro

DIRECTIONS

1. Heat the oil in a large pot over medium heat, and cook the onion, ginger, garlic, and fenugreek until onion is tender.
2. Mix the lentils, squash, and cilantro into the pot. Stir in the water, coconut milk, and tomato paste. Season with curry powder, cayenne pepper, nutmeg, salt, and pepper. Bring to a boil, reduce heat to low, and simmer 30 minutes, or until lentils and squash are tender.

VEGETARIAN MOUSSAKA

Servings: 7 | Prep: 30m | Cooks: 1h30m | Total: 2h

NUTRITION FACTS

Calories: 239.8 | Carbohydrates: 25.5g | Protein: 10.2g | Cholesterol: 58.2mg | Sodium: 425.7mg

INGREDIENTS

- 1 eggplant, thinly sliced
- 2 tablespoons chopped fresh parsley

- 1 tablespoon olive oil, or more as needed

- 1 large zucchini, thinly sliced

- 2 medium (2-1/4" to 3" dia, raw)s potatoes, thinly sliced

- 1 onion, sliced

- 1 clove garlic, chopped

- 1 tablespoon white vinegar

- 1 (14.5 ounce) can whole peeled tomatoes, chopped

- 1/2 (14.5 ounce) can lentils, drained with

- salt and ground black pepper to taste

- 1 cup crumbled feta cheese

- 1 1/2 tablespoons butter

- 2 tablespoons all-purpose flour

- 1 1/4 cups milk

- 1 pinch ground black pepper to taste

- 1 pinch ground nutmeg

- 1 egg, beaten

liquid reserved

- 1 teaspoon dried oregano
- 1/4 cup grated Parmesan cheese

DIRECTIONS

1. Sprinkle eggplant slices with salt and set aside for 30 minutes. Rinse and pat dry.
2. Preheat oven to 375 degrees F (190 degrees C).
3. Heat oil in a large skillet over medium-high heat. Rinse and pat eggplant dry. Cook eggplant and zucchini in hot oil until lightly browned on both sides, about 3 minutes per side; remove with a slotted spoon to drain on a paper towel-lined plate, reserving as much oil as possible in the skillet
4. Adding more oil to skillet as needed and let it get hot. Cook potato slices in hot oil until browned, 3 to 5 minutes per side; remove with slotted spoon and drain on a paper towel-lined plate, again reserving oil in the skillet.
5. Saute onion and garlic in reserved oil until lightly browned, 5 to 7 minutes. Pour in vinegar, bring to a boil, and reduce heat to medium-low; cook until liquid is reduced in volume and thick. Stir in tomatoes, lentils, 1/2 the juice from lentils, oregano and parsley. Cover, reduce heat to medium-low, and simmer 15 minutes.
6. Layer about 1/3 of the eggplant, 1/3 of the zucchini, 1/2 the potatoes, 1/2 the onions, and 1/2 the feta into a 13x9-inch baking dish. Pour tomato mixture over vegetables; repeat layering, finishing with a layer of eggplant and zucchini.
7. Cover and bake in preheated oven for 25 minutes.

8. Stir butter, flour, and milk together in a small saucepan; bring to a slow boil, whisking constantly until thick and smooth. Season with pepper and nutmeg; stir. Remove from heat, cool for 5 minutes, and stir in beaten egg.
9. Pour sauce over vegetables and sprinkle with Parmesan cheese. Bake, uncovered, for another 25 to 30 minutes.

PORK CHALUPAS

Servings: 16 | Prep: 15m | Cooks: 9h | Total: 9h15m

NUTRITION FACTS

Calories: 474.3 | Carbohydrates: 57.8g | Protein: 26.4g | Cholesterol: 45.2mg | Sodium: 1622.2mg

INGREDIENTS

- 1 (4 pound) pork shoulder roast
- 1 pound dried pinto beans
- 3 (4 ounce) cans diced green chile peppers
- 2 tablespoons chili powder
- 2 tablespoons salt
- 2 tablespoons dried oregano
- 2 tablespoons garlic powder
- 16 eaches flour tortillas

- 2 tablespoons ground cumin

DIRECTIONS

1. Place the roast inside a slow cooker coated with cooking spray. In a separate bowl, stir together the beans, 2 cans of the chile peppers, chili powder, cumin, salt, oregano, and garlic powder. Pour the whole mixture over the roast, and add enough water so that the roast is mostly covered. Jiggle the roast a little to get some of the liquid underneath.
2. Cover, and cook on Low for 8 to 9 hours. Check after about 5 hours to make sure the beans have not absorbed all of the liquid. Add more water if necessary 1 cup at a time. Use just enough to keep the beans from drying out.
3. When the roast is fork-tender, remove it from the slow cooker, and place on a cutting board. Remove any bone and fat, then shred with forks. Return to the slow cooker, and stir in the remaining can of green chilies. Heat through, and serve with flour tortillas and your favorite toppings.

MEXICAN QUESADILLA CASSEROLE
Servings: 8 | Prep: 15m | Cooks: 25m | Total: 45m | Additional: 5m

NUTRITION FACTS

Calories: 493 | Carbohydrates: 50.1g | Fat: 21.2g | Protein: 26.6g | Cholesterol: 65mg | Sodium: 1423mg

INGREDIENTS

- cooking spray
- 1 pound ground beef
- 1/2 cup chopped onion
- 1 (15 ounce) can tomato sauce
- 1 (15 ounce) can black beans, rinsed and drained
- 1 (14.5 ounce) can diced tomatoes with lime juice and cilantro (such as RO*TEL®)
- 1 (8.75 ounce) can whole kernel sweet corn, drained
- 2 teaspoons chili powder
- 1 teaspoon ground cumin
- 1 teaspoon minced garlic
- 1/2 teaspoon dried oregano
- 1/2 teaspoon red pepper flakes
- 6 flour tortillas
- 2 cups shredded Cheddar cheese

- 1 (4.5 ounce) can chopped green chiles, drained

DIRECTIONS

1. Preheat oven to 350 degrees F (175 degrees C). Prepare a 13x9-inch baking dish with cooking spray.
2. Heat a large skillet over medium-high heat. Cook and stir beef and onion in the hot skillet until beef is completely browned, 5 to 7 minutes; drain and discard grease.
3. Stir tomato sauce, black beans, diced tomatoes with lime juice and cilantro, corn, and chopped green chiles into the ground beef mixture; season with chili powder, cumin, garlic, oregano, and red pepper flakes. Reduce heat to low and cook mixture at a simmer for 5 minutes.
4. Spread about 1/2 cup beef mixture into the bottom of the prepared baking dish; top with 3 tortillas, overlapping as needed. Spread another 1/2 cup beef mixture over the tortillas. Sprinkle 1 cup Cheddar cheese over beef. Finish with layers of remaining tortillas, beef mixture, and Cheddar cheese, respectively.
5. Bake in preheated oven until heated throughout and the cheese is melted, about 15 minutes. Cool 5 minutes before serving.

EASY CHICKEN FAJITA SOUP
Servings: 10 | Prep: 20m | Cooks: 55m | Total: 1h15m

NUTRITION FACTS

Calories: 142.7 | Carbohydrates: 15.6g | Protein: 12.4g | Cholesterol: 24.4mg | Sodium: 714mg

INGREDIENTS

- 2 tablespoons vegetable oil

- 1 pound skinless, boneless chicken breasts, cut into strips

- 1 (1.27 ounce) packet fajita seasoning

- 1 red bell pepper, cut into thin strips

- 1 green bell pepper, cut into thin strips

- 1 poblano pepper, cut into thin strips

- 1 large onion, cut into thin strips

- 1 (14.5 ounce) can fire roasted diced tomatoes

- 1 (15 ounce) can seasoned black beans

- 1 (14 ounce) can chicken broth

- 1 dash hot sauce

- 1 pinch salt and pepper to taste

DIRECTIONS

1. Heat oil in a large soup pot over medium heat. Place chicken in the hot oil; cook, stirring only occasionally, until brown, about 10 minutes. Sprinkle fajita seasoning over the browned chicken and stir well to coat. Add the red and green bell pepper, poblano pepper, and onion to the seasoned chicken. Stir and cook over medium heat until the vegetables are soft, about 10 minutes.
2. Pour the fire roasted tomatoes, black beans, and chicken broth into the pot with the chicken and vegetables. Bring the soup to a boil over high heat, then reduce the heat to medium-low, and simmer uncovered for 30 minutes, stirring occasionally.
3. Season the soup with hot sauce, salt, and pepper to taste before serving.

CREAMY ITALIAN WHITE BEAN SOUP
Servings: 4 | Prep: 20m | Cooks: 30m | Total: 50m

NUTRITION FACTS

Calories: 244.7 | Carbohydrates: 38.1g | Protein: 12g | Cholesterol: 2.4mg | Sodium: 1014.4mg

INGREDIENTS

- 1 tablespoon vegetable oil
- 1 onion, chopped
- 1/4 teaspoon ground black pepper
- 1/8 teaspoon dried thyme

- 1 stalk celery, chopped
- 1 clove garlic, minced
- 2 (16 ounce) cans white kidney beans, rinsed and drained
- 1 (14 ounce) can chicken broth
- 2 cups water
- 1 bunch fresh spinach, rinsed and thinly sliced
- 1 tablespoon lemon juice

DIRECTIONS

1. In a large saucepan, heat oil. Cook onion and celery in oil for 5 to 8 minutes, or until tender. Add garlic, and cook for 30 seconds, continually stirring. Stir in beans, chicken broth, pepper, thyme and 2 cups water. Bring to a boil, reduce heat, and then simmer for 15 minutes.
2. With slotted spoon, remove 2 cups of the bean and vegetable mixture from soup and set aside.
3. In blender at low speed, blend remaining soup in small batches until smooth, (it helps to remove the center piece of the blender lid to allow steam to escape.) Once blended pour soup back into stock pot and stir in reserved beans.
4. Bring to a boil, occasionally stirring. Stir in spinach and cook 1 minute or until spinach is wilted. Stir in lemon juice and remove from heat and serve with fresh grated Parmesan cheese on top.

CALICO BEAN CASSEROLE

Servings: 6 | Prep: 20m | Cooks: 30m | Total: 50m

NUTRITION FACTS

Calories: 617.1 | Carbohydrates: 69.2g | Protein: 27.6g | Cholesterol: 74.9mg | Sodium: 1089.1mg

INGREDIENTS

- 1 (15 ounce) can kidney beans, undrained
- 1 (16 ounce) can baked beans with pork
- 1 (15 ounce) can butter beans, undrained
- 1/2 cup ketchup
- 2 teaspoons white vinegar
- 1 tablespoon dry mustard
- 3/4 cup packed brown sugar
- 1 pound lean ground beef
- 4 ounces bacon, chopped
- 1/2 cup chopped onion
- salt to taste
- ground black pepper to taste

DIRECTIONS

1. Preheat oven to 350 degrees F (175 degrees C).
2. In a large skillet over medium heat, fry the ground beef, bacon and onion together until ground beef is no longer

pink. Drain fat.
3. In a large mixing bowl, combine the kidney beans, baked beans with pork and butter beans. Stir in the ketchup, white vinegar, dry mustard, brown sugar and cook beef mixture. Mix thoroughly, adding salt and pepper to taste.
4. Pour the bean and meat mixture into a 9x13 inch baking dish. Bake in preheated oven for 30 to 40 minutes.

PUMPKIN CHILI
Servings: 8 | Prep: 20m | Cooks: 1h | Total: 1h20m

NUTRITION FACTS

Calories: 408.5 | Carbohydrates: 37.6g | Protein: 28.2g | Cholesterol: 68.6mg | Sodium: 924.2mg

INGREDIENTS

- 2 pounds ground beef
- 1 large onion, diced
- 1 green bell pepper, diced
- 1 (28 ounce) can peeled and diced tomatoes with juice
- 1/2 cup canned pumpkin puree
- 1 tablespoon pumpkin pie spice

- 2 (15 ounce) cans kidney beans, drained
- 1 (46 fluid ounce) can tomato juice
- 1 tablespoon chili powder
- 1/4 cup white sugar

DIRECTIONS

1. In a large pot over medium heat, cook beef until brown; drain. Stir in onion and bell pepper and cook 5 minutes. Stir in beans, tomato juice, diced tomatoes and pumpkin puree. Season with pumpkin pie spice, chili powder and sugar. Simmer 1 hour.

CROCK-POT CHICKEN CHILI
Servings: 5 | Prep: 10m | Cooks: 6h | Total: 6h10m

NUTRITION FACTS

Calories: 385.6 | Carbohydrates: 62.9g | Protein: 28.8g | Cholesterol: 36.9mg | Sodium: 1338.2mg

INGREDIENTS

- 1 (16 ounce) jar green salsa (salsa verde)
- 1 (16 ounce) can diced tomatoes with green chile peppers
- 1 onion, chopped
- 1/2 teaspoon dried oregano

- 2 (15 ounce) cans white beans, drained
- 1 (14.5 ounce) can chicken broth
- 1 (14 ounce) can corn, drained
- 1/4 teaspoon ground cumin
- 1 pinch salt and ground black pepper to taste
- 3 eaches skinless, boneless chicken breasts

DIRECTIONS

1. Mix green salsa, diced tomatoes with green chile peppers, white beans, chicken broth, corn, onion, oregano, cumin, salt, and black pepper together in a slow cooker. Lay chicken breasts atop the mixture.
2. Cook on Low until the chicken shreds easily with 2 forks, 6 to 8 hours.
3. Remove chicken to a cutting board and shred completely; return to chili in slow cooker and stir.

TEXAS CAVIAR

Servings: 16 | Prep: 15m | Cooks: 1h | Total: 1h15m | Additional: 1h

NUTRITION FACTS

Calories: 107.1 | Carbohydrates: 11.8g | Protein: 3.5g | Cholesterol: 0mg | Sodium: 414.7mg

INGREDIENTS

- 1/2 onion, chopped
- 1 green bell pepper, chopped
- 1 bunch green onions, chopped
- 2 jalapeno peppers, chopped
- 1 tablespoon minced garlic
- 1 pint cherry tomatoes, quartorod
- 1 (8 ounce) bottle zesty Italian dressing
- 1 (15 ounce) can black beans, drained
- 1 (15 ounce) can black-eyed peas, drained
- 1/2 teaspoon ground coriander
- 1 bunch chopped fresh cilantro

DIRECTIONS

1. In a large bowl, mix together onion, green bell pepper, green onions, jalapeno peppers, garlic, cherry tomatoes, zesty Italian dressing, black beans, black-eyed peas and

coriander. Cover and chill in the refrigerator approximately 2 hours. Toss with desired amount of fresh cilantro to serve.

MEATIEST VEGETARIAN CHILI FROM YOUR SLOW COOKER

Servings: 8 | Prep: 30m | Cooks: 6h10m | Total: 6h40m

NUTRITION FACTS

Calories: 454.5 | Carbohydrates: 58.2g | Protein: 21.2g | Cholesterol: 0mg | Sodium: 1645.5mg

INGREDIENTS

- 1/2 cup olive oil
- 4 onions, chopped
- 2 green bell peppers, seeded and chopped
- 2 red bell peppers, seeded and chopped
- 4 cloves garlic, minced
- 2 teaspoons salt
- 1/2 teaspoon ground black pepper
- 2 teaspoons ground cumin
- 6 tablespoons chili powder
- 2 tablespoons dried oregano

- 1 (14 ounce) package firm tofu, drained and cubed

- 4 (15.5 ounce) cans black beans, drained

- 2 (15 ounce) cans crushed tomatoes

- 2 tablespoons distilled white vinegar

- 1 tablespoon liquid hot pepper sauce, such as Tabasco

DIRECTIONS

1. Heat the olive oil in a large skillet over medium-high heat. Add the onions; cook and stir until they start to become soft. Add the green peppers, red peppers, garlic and tofu; cook and stir until vegetables are lightly browned and tender, the whole process should take about 10 minutes.
2. Pour the black beans into the slow cooker and set to Low. Stir in the vegetables and tomatoes. Season with salt, pepper, cumin, chili powder, oregano, vinegar and hot pepper sauce. Stir gently and cover. Cook on LOW for 6 to 8 hours.

WASHABINAROS CHILI
Servings: 8 | Prep: 20m | Cooks: 3h | Total: 3h20m

NUTRITION FACTS

Calories: 542.9 | Carbohydrates: 52g | Protein: 28.4g | Cholesterol: 51.1mg | Sodium: 1679.6mg

INGREDIENTS

- 4 tablespoons vegetable oil, divided
- 2 onions, chopped
- 4 cloves garlic, minced
- 1 pound ground beef
- 3/4 pound spicy Italian sausage, casing removed
- 1 (14.5 ounce) can peeled and diced tomatoes with juice
- 1 tablespoon ground cumin
- 1/4 cup brown sugar
- 1 teaspoon dried oregano
- 1 teaspoon cayenne pepper
- 1 teaspoon ground coriander
- 1 teaspoon salt

- 1 (12 fluid ounce) can or bottle dark beer
- 1 cup strong brewed coffee
- 2 (6 ounce) cans tomato paste
- 1 (14 ounce) can beef broth
- 1/4 cup chili powder
- 1 tablespoon wasabi paste
- 3 (15 ounce) cans kidney beans
- 2 Anaheim chile peppers, chopped
- 1 serrano pepper, chopped
- 1 habanero pepper, sliced

DIRECTIONS

1. Place 2 tablespoons of oil in a large pot and place the pot over medium heat. Cook and stir the onions, garlic, beef and sausage until meats are browned. Pour in the tomatoes, beer, coffee, tomato paste and broth. Season with chili powder, cumin, sugar, oregano, cayenne, coriander, salt and wasabi. Stir in one can of beans, bring to a boil, then reduce heat, cover and simmer.
2. In a large skillet over medium heat, heat remaining oil. Cook Anaheim, serrano and habanero peppers in oil until just tender, 5 to 10 minutes. Stir into the pot and simmer 2 hours.

3. Stir in remaining 2 cans of beans and cook 45 minutes more.

EASY HOMEMADE CHILI

Servings: 6 | Prep: 10m | Cooks: 20m | Total: 30m

NUTRITION FACTS

Calories: 394.2 | Carbohydrates: 48.8g | Protein: 30.6g | Cholesterol: 45.9mg | Sodium: 525.6mg

INGREDIENTS

- 1 pound ground beef
- 1 onion, chopped
- 1 (14.5 ounce) can stewed tomatoes
- 1 (15 ounce) can tomato sauce
- 1 (15 ounce) can kidney beans
- 1 1/2 cups water
- 1 pinch chili powder
- 1 pinch garlic powder
- salt and pepper to taste

DIRECTIONS

1. In a large saucepan over medium heat, combine the beef and onion and saute until meat is browned and onion is tender. Add the stewed tomatoes with juice, tomato sauce, beans and water.
2. Season with the chili powder, garlic powder, salt and ground black pepper to taste. Bring to a boil, reduce heat to low, cover and let simmer for 15 minutes.

CHILI RICK'S

Servings: 20 | Prep: 30m | Cooks: 2h30m | Total: 3h

NUTRITION FACTS

Calories: 507.9 | Carbohydrates: 43.5g | Protein: 28.1g | Cholesterol: 75.3mg | Sodium: 2080.1mg

INGREDIENTS

- 2 (29 ounce) cans tomato sauce
- 3 pounds lean ground beef
- 2 (28 ounce) cans peeled and diced tomatoes
- 1 (32 ounce) bottle hickory smoke barbeque sauce
- 2 cups diced onion
- 1/2 cup chili powder
- 1 tablespoon Italian seasoning
- 4 (15.25 ounce) cans kidney beans,

- 1 pound bacon, diced

- 2 pounds spicy sausage

- undrained

- 2 (1 ounce) squares unsweetened chocolate, chopped

DIRECTIONS

1. In a large pot or Dutch oven over medium heat, combine tomato sauce, tomatoes, onion and Italian seasoning.
2. In a large skillet over medium heat, cook bacon until slightly crisp. Drain and stir into the pot.
3. In the same skillet over medium heat, cook sausage until brown. Drain and stir into the pot.
4. In the same skillet over medium heat, cook the beef until brown. Drain and stir into the pot.
5. Stir the barbeque sauce and chili powder into the pot; taste and adjust seasonings. Stir in the kidney beans and chocolate and simmer until flavors are well blended. Serve.

SPICED QUINOA

Servings: 4 | Prep: 20m | Cooks: 25m | Total: 45m

NUTRITION FACTS

Calories: 439.8 | Carbohydrates: 64.8g | Protein: 14.8g | Cholesterol: 0.3mg | Sodium: 851.1mg

INGREDIENTS

- 1 tablespoon olive oil
- 1 small onion, chopped
- 1 clove garlic, minced
- 3/4 cup quinoa
- 1 1/2 teaspoons curry powder
- 1/2 teaspoon salt
- 1/2 teaspoon black pepper

- 1/2 teaspoon cumin
- 1/4 teaspoon cinnamon
- 1 1/2 cups chicken stock
- 1 (14 ounce) can garbanzo beans, drained and rinsed
- 1/2 cup toasted pine nuts
- 1/2 cup raisins, soaked in hot water and drained

DIRECTIONS

1. Stir together the olive oil, onion, and garlic in a saucepan over medium heat until the onion has softened and turned translucent, about 5 minutes. Stir in the quinoa, curry powder, salt, pepper, cumin, cinnamon, and chicken stock. Bring to a boil, then reduce heat to medium-low, cover, and simmer 20 minutes until the quinoa is tender.
2. Once the quinoa has finished cooking, stir in the drained garbanzo beans, toasted pine nuts, and raisins. Serve warm or cold.

BEST BEEF ENCHILADAS

Servings: 8 | Prep: 25m | Cooks: 20m | Total: 45m

NUTRITION FACTS

Calories: 583.2 | Carbohydrates: 46.1g | Protein: 33g | Cholesterol: 93.7mg | Sodium: 1216.3mg

INGREDIENTS

- 2 pounds ground beef
- 1/4 onion, finely chopped
- 1 cup shredded Cheddar cheese
- 1/2 cup sour cream
- 2 1/2 cups enchilada sauce
- 1 1/2 teaspoons chili powder
- 1 clove garlic, minced
- 1/2 teaspoon salt

- 1 tablespoon dried parsley
- 1 tablespoon taco seasoning
- 1 teaspoon dried oregano
- 1/2 teaspoon ground black pepper
- 8 eaches flour tortillas
- 1 (15 ounce) can black beans, rinsed and drained
- 1 (4 ounce) can sliced black olives, drained
- 1/4 cup shredded Cheddar cheese

DIRECTIONS

1. Preheat oven to 350 degrees F (175 degrees C).
2. Cook and stir ground beef with onion in a skillet over medium heat until meat is crumbly and no longer pink, about 10 minutes. Drain grease. Stir 1 cup Cheddar cheese, sour cream, parsley, taco seasoning, oregano, and black pepper into the ground beef until cheese has melted. Mix in enchilada sauce, chili powder, garlic, and salt; bring to a simmer, reduce heat to low, and simmer until meat sauce is slightly thickened, about 5 minutes.
3. Lay a tortilla onto a work surface and spoon about 1/4 cup of meat sauce down the center of the tortilla. Top meat sauce with 1 tablespoon black beans and a sprinkling of black olives. Roll the tortilla up, enclosing the filling, and lay

seam-side down into a 9x13-inch baking dish. Repeat with remaining tortillas. Spoon any remaining meat sauce over the enchiladas and scatter any remaining black beans and black olives over the top. Sprinkle tortillas with 1/4 cup Cheddar cheese.
4. Bake in the preheated oven until cheese topping is melted and enchiladas and sauce are bubbling, 20 to 22 minutes. Let stand 5 minutes before serving.

SPINACH LENTIL SOUP

Servings: 8 | Prep: 15m | Cooks: 35m | Total: 50m

NUTRITION FACTS

Calories: 150 | Carbohydrates: 22.7g | Fat: 2.4g | Protein: 10.1g | Cholesterol: 10mg | Sodium: 190mg

INGREDIENTS

- 1/3 cup uncooked white rice
- 2/3 cup water
- 1 teaspoon vegetable oil
- 4 ounces turkey kielbasa, chopped
- 1/2 teaspoon crushed red pepper flakes
- 6 cups water
- 2 cups reduced sodium chicken broth
- 1 cup dry lentils

- 1 onion, minced
- 1 (10 ounce) bag fresh spinach, torn
- 1 carrot, chopped

DIRECTIONS

1. In a pot, bring the rice and water to a boil. Reduce heat to low, cover, and simmer 20 minutes.
2. Heat the oil in a large pot over medium heat, and cook the turkey kielbasa until lightly browned. Mix in onion and carrot, and season with red pepper. Cook and stir until tender. Pour in the water and broth, and mix in lentils. Bring to a boil, reduce heat to low, and simmer 25 minutes.
3. Stir the cooked rice and spinach into the soup, and continue cooking 5 minutes before serving.

BLACK BEAN CHILI

Servings: 8 | Prep: 20m | Cooks: 20m | Total: 40m

NUTRITION FACTS

Calories: 164.3 | Carbohydrates: 28g | Protein: 9g | Cholesterol: 0.9mg | Sodium: 897.4mg

INGREDIENTS

- 1 tablespoon olive oil
- 1 teaspoon ground black pepper

- 1 onion, chopped
- 2 red bell pepper, seeded and chopped
- 1 jalapeno pepper, seeded and minced
- 10 fresh mushrooms, quartered
- 6 roma (plum) tomatoes, diced
- 1 cup fresh corn kernels
- 1 teaspoon ground cumin
- 1 tablespoon chili powder
- 2 (15 ounce) cans black beans, drained and rinsed
- 1 1/2 cups chicken broth or vegetable broth
- 1 teaspoon salt

DIRECTIONS

1. Heat oil in a large saucepan over medium-high heat. Saute the onion, red bell peppers, jalapeno, mushrooms, tomatoes and corn for 10 minutes or until the onions are translucent. Season with black pepper, cumin, and chili powder. Stir in

the black beans, chicken or vegetable broth, and salt. Bring to a boil.
2. Reduce heat to medium low. Remove 1 1/2 cups of the soup to food processor or blender; puree and stir the bean mixture back into the soup. Serve hot by itself or over rice.

SPICY BLACK BEAN CAKES

Servings: 8 | Prep: 20m | Cooks: 15m | Total: 35m

NUTRITION FACTS

Calories: 218.6 | Carbohydrates: 31.3g | Protein: 9.4g | Cholesterol: 29.1mg | Sodium: 519.7mg

INGREDIENTS

- 1/2 cup reduced fat sour cream
- 2 teaspoons fresh lime juice
- 1 small fresh jalapeno pepper, minced
- 1 pinch salt to taste
- 2 fresh jalapeno peppers, finely diced
- 1 tablespoon ground cumin
- 2 (14.5 ounce) cans black beans, drained and rinsed
- 1 pinch salt and black pepper to taste

- 2 tablespoons olive oil, divided
- 4 green onions, thinly sliced
- 6 cloves garlic, pressed
- 2 cups grated raw sweet potato
- 1 egg, lightly beaten
- 1/2 cup plain dried bread crumbs

DIRECTIONS

1. To prepare lime sour cream, mix the sour cream, lime juice, 1 small minced jalapeno, and salt together in a small bowl. Cover, and refrigerate.
2. Heat 1 tablespoon olive oil in a small skillet over medium heat. Cook green onions until softened, about 1 minute. Stir in garlic, 2 diced jalapenos, and cumin; cook until fragrant, about 30 seconds.
3. Transfer contents of skillet to a large bowl. Stir in black beans, and mash with a fork. Season with salt and pepper to taste. Mix in sweet potatoes, egg, and bread crumbs. Divide into 8 balls, and flatten into patties.
4. In the oven, set cooking rack about 4 inches from heat source. Set oven to broil. Lightly grease baking sheet with 1 tablespoon oil.
5. Place bean patties on baking sheet, and broil 8 to 10 minutes. Turn cakes over, and broil until crispy, about 3 minutes more. Serve with lime sour cream.

EASY HUMMUS

Servings: 16 | Prep: 5m | Cooks: 0m | Total: 5m

NUTRITION FACTS

Calories: 23.4 | Carbohydrates: 4.5g | Protein: 1g | Cholesterol: 0mg | Sodium: 52.6mg

INGREDIENTS

- 1 (15 ounce) can garbanzo beans, drained, liquid reserved
- 2 ounces fresh jalapeno pepper, sliced
- 1/2 teaspoon ground cumin
- 2 tablespoons lemon juice
- 3 cloves garlic, minced

DIRECTIONS

1. In a blender or food processor, combine garbanzo beans, jalapeno, cumin, lemon juice, garlic and 1 tablespoon of the reserved bean liquid. Blend until smooth.

MINESTRONE SOUP
Servings: 6 | Prep: 20m | Cooks: 1h25m | Total: 1h45m

NUTRITION FACTS

Calories: 484 | Carbohydrates: 53.9g | Fat: 23g | Protein: 17.9g | Cholesterol: 16mg | Sodium: 2020mg

INGREDIENTS

- 2 tablespoons olive oil
- 3 ounces chopped pancetta
- 1 onion, diced
- 1 cup diced celery
- 1 (15 ounce) can garbanzo beans, drained
- 1 teaspoon red pepper flakes, or to taste
- 1 teaspoon Italian seasoning
- 2 teaspoons salt

- 4 cloves garlic, minced
- 4 cups chicken broth
- 2 cups water, plus more as needed
- 1 (28 ounce) can plum tomatoes, crushed fine
- 1 cup cranberry beans, shelled
- 2 cups chopped cabbage, or more to taste
- 1 bunch Swiss chard, chopped
- 2/3 cup ditalini pasta
- salt and ground black pepper
- 1/4 cup extra virgin olive oil, for drizzling
- 1/4 cup finely grated Parmigiano-Reggiano cheese
- 1/4 cup chopped fresh Italian flat-leaf parsley

DIRECTIONS

1. Heat 2 tablespoons olive oil in large stock pot over medium-high heat. Add pancetta; cook and stir until it begins to brown, 2 to 3 minutes. Stir in onions and celery; cook and stir until onions start to turn translucent, about 3 minutes. Stir in minced garlic and cook for another minute.

2. Pour chicken broth, water, and plum tomatoes into the pancetta and onion mixture. Bring to a simmer.
3. Stir cranberry beans, cabbage, garbanzo beans, red pepper flakes, Italian seasoning, and 2 teaspoons salt into broth mixture. Bring to a simmer and cook until cranberry beans are tender, adding more water as needed if the soup becomes too thick, about 45 minutes.
4. Stir in Swiss chard and simmer until softened, about 15 minutes. Season with salt and black pepper to taste.
5. Stir in pasta and increase heat to medium-high and simmer until pasta is tender, about 15 minutes. Ladle into bowls and top with extra virgin olive oil, Parmigiano-Reggiano cheese, and Italian parsley.

SWISS CHARD WITH GARBANZO BEANS AND FRESH TOMATOES

Servings: 4 | Prep: 10m | Cooks: 15m | Total: 25m

NUTRITION FACTS

Calories: 121.7 | Carbohydrates: 13.3g | Protein: 3.2g | Cholesterol: 0mg | Sodium: 253.2mg

INGREDIENTS

- 2 tablespoons olive oil
- 1 pinch salt and pepper to taste
- 1 shallot, chopped
- 1 bunch red Swiss chard, rinsed and chopped

- 2 eaches green onions, chopped
- 1 tomato, sliced
- 1/2 cup garbanzo beans, drained
- 1/2 lemon, juiced

DIRECTIONS

1. Heat olive oil in a large skillet. Stir in shallot and green onions; cook and stir for 3 to 5 minutes, or until soft and fragrant. Stir in garbanzo beans, and season with salt and pepper; heat through. Place chard in pan, and cook until wilted. Add tomato slices, squeeze lemon juice over greens, and heat through. Plate, and season with salt and pepper to taste.

UNSLOPPY JOES

Servings: 8 | Prep: 15m | Cooks: 15m | Total: 30m

NUTRITION FACTS

Calories: 204.4 | Carbohydrates: 35.6g | Protein: 7.8g | Cholesterol: 0mg | Sodium: 488.8mg

INGREDIENTS

- 1 tablespoon olive oil
- 1/2 cup chopped onion
- 1/2 cup chopped celery
- 1/2 cup chopped carrots
- 1/2 cup chopped green bell pepper
- 1 clove garlic, minced
- 1 (14.5 ounce) can diced tomatoes
- 1 1/2 tablespoons chili powder
- 1 tablespoon tomato paste
- 1 tablespoon distilled white vinegar
- 1 teaspoon ground black pepper
- 1 (15 ounce) can kidney beans, drained and rinsed
- 8 eaches kaiser rolls

DIRECTIONS

1. Heat olive oil in a large skillet over medium heat. Add onion, celery, carrot, green pepper, and garlic: saute until tender. Stir in tomatoes, chili powder, tomato paste, vinegar, and pepper. Cover, reduce heat, and simmer 10 minutes.
2. Stir in kidney beans, and cook an additional 5 minutes.
3. Cut a 1/4 inch slice off the top of each kaiser roll; set aside. Hollow out the center of each roll, leaving about 1/2 inch thick shells; reserve the inside of rolls for other uses.
4. Spoon bean mixture evenly into rolls and replace tops. Serve immediately.

MEXICAN PASTA

Servings: 4 | Prep: 5m | Cooks: 15m | Total: 20m

NUTRITION FACTS

Calories: 357.7 | Carbohydrates: 59.5g | Protein: 10.3g | Cholesterol: 0mg | Sodium: 588.9mg

INGREDIENTS

- 1/2 pound seashell pasta
- 1 (14.5 ounce) can peeled and diced tomatoes
- 2 tablespoons olive oil
- 1/4 cup salsa
- 2 onions, chopped
- 1/4 cup sliced black olives

- 1 green bell pepper, chopped
- ½ cup sweet corn kernels
- 1 (15 ounce) can black beans, drained
- 1 1/2 tablespoons taco seasoning mix
- salt and pepper to taste

DIRECTIONS

1. Bring a large pot of lightly salted water to a boil. Add pasta and cook for 8 to 10 minutes or until al dente; drain.
2. While pasta is cooking, heat olive oil over medium heat in a large skillet. Cook onions and pepper in oil until lightly browned, 10 minutes. Stir in corn and heat through. Stir in black beans, tomatoes, salsa, olives, taco seasoning and salt and pepper and cook until thoroughly heated, 5 minutes.
3. Toss sauce with cooked pasta and serve.

VEGGIE VEGETARIAN CHILI

Servings: 16 | Prep: 15m | Cooks: 40m | Total: 55m

NUTRITION FACTS

Calories: 98.4 | Carbohydrates: 18.5g | Protein: 4.4g | Cholesterol: 0mg | Sodium: 277.9mg

INGREDIENTS

- 1 tablespoon vegetable oil
- 3 cloves garlic, minced
- 1 cup chopped onion
- 1 cup chopped carrots
- 1 cup chopped green bell pepper
- 1 cup chopped red bell pepper
- 2 tablespoons chili powder
- 1 (15 ounce) can black beans, undrained
- 1 (15 ounce) can kidney beans, undrained
- 1 (15 ounce) can pinto beans, undrained
- 1 (15 ounce) can whole kernel corn, drained
- 1 tablespoon cumin
- 1 1/2 tablespoons dried oregano
- 1 1/2 tablespoons dried basil

- 1 1/2 cups chopped fresh mushrooms
- 1 (28 ounce) can whole peeled tomatoes with liquid, chopped

- 1/2 tablespoon garlic powder

DIRECTIONS

1. Heat the oil in a large pot over medium heat. Cook and stir the garlic, onion, and carrots in the pot until tender. Mix in the green bell pepper and red bell pepper. Season with chili powder. Continue cooking 5 minutes, or until peppers are tender.
2. Mix the mushrooms into the pot. Stir in the tomatoes with liquid, black beans with liquid, kidney beans with liquid, pinto beans with liquid, and corn. Season with cumin, oregano, basil, and garlic powder. Bring to a boil. Reduce heat to medium, cover, and cook 20 minutes, stirring occasionally.

LEBANESE-STYLE RED LENTIL SOUP

Servings: 8 | Prep: 20m | Cooks: 30m | Total: 50m

NUTRITION FACTS

Calories: 276.4 | Carbohydrates: 39.1g | Protein: 16.7g | Cholesterol: 0.6mg | Sodium: 524.1mg

INGREDIENTS

- 6 cups chicken stock
- 1 tablespoon ground cumin
- 1 pound red lentils
- 1/2 teaspoon cayenne pepper

- 3 tablespoons olive oil
- 1 tablespoon minced garlic
- 1 large onion, chopped
- 1/2 cup chopped cilantro
- 3/4 cup fresh lemon juice

DIRECTIONS

1. Bring chicken stock and lentils to a boil in a large saucepan over high heat, then reduce heat to medium-low, cover, and simmer for 20 minutes.
2. Meanwhile, heat olive oil in a skillet over medium heat. Stir in garlic and onion, and cook until the onion has softened and turned translucent, about 3 minutes.
3. Stir onions into the lentils and season with cumin and cayenne. Continue simmering until the lentils are tender, about 10 minutes.
4. Carefully puree the soup in a standing blender, or with a stick blender until smooth. Stir in cilantro and lemon juice before serving.

SLOW COOKER HOMEMADE BEANS
Servings: 12 | Prep: 20m | Cooks: 10h | Total: 10h20m

NUTRITION FACTS

Calories: 296.1 | Carbohydrates: 57g | Protein: 12.4g | Cholesterol: 5mg | Sodium: 1312.2mg

INGREDIENTS

- 3 cups dry navy beans, soaked overnight or boiled for one hour
- 1 1/2 cups ketchup
- 1 1/2 cups water
- 1/4 cup molasses
- 1 large onion, chopped
- 1 tablespoon dry mustard
- 1 tablespoon salt
- 6 slices thick cut bacon, cut into 1 inch pieces
- 1 cup brown sugar

DIRECTIONS

1. Drain soaking liquid from beans, and place them in a Slow Cooker.
2. Stir ketchup, water, molasses, onion, mustard, salt, bacon, and brown sugar into the beans until well mixed.
3. Cover, and cook on LOW for 8 to 10 hours, stirring occasionally if possible, though not necessary.

SUE'S TACO SALAD

Servings: 6 | Prep: 15m | Cooks: 15m | Total: 30m

NUTRITION FACTS

Calories: 626.1 | Carbohydrates: 33.2g | Protein: 28.2g | Cholesterol: 91.7mg | Sodium: 1125mg

INGREDIENTS

- 1 pound lean ground beef
- 1 (1 ounce) package taco seasoning mix
- 1/2 (14.5 ounce) package nacho-flavor tortilla chips
- 2 cups shredded Cheddar cheese
- 1/2 cup ranch-style salad dressing
- 1 chopped tomato
- 1 cup chopped lettuce
- 1/4 cup chopped green onion

- 1/2 (15 ounce) can kidney beans, drained

DIRECTIONS

1. Place ground beef in a large, deep skillet. Cook over medium-high heat, stirring to crumble until well done; drain. Stir in taco seasoning mix. Set aside to cool.
2. Place chips into a large bowl, and crush into bite-size pieces. Combine with seasoned meat, cheese, beans, tomatoes, lettuce, and green onions. Pour dressing over all, and toss to coat.

CHICKPEA SALAD WITH RED ONION AND TOMATO

Servings: 4 | Prep: 10m | Cooks: 2h | Total: 2h | Additional: 2h

NUTRITION FACTS

Calories: 262.3 | Carbohydrates: 33.3g | Protein: 7.3g | Cholesterol: 0mg | Sodium: 404.4mg

INGREDIENTS

- 19 ounces garbanzo beans, drained
- 2 tablespoons red onion, chopped
- 1/2 cup chopped parsley
- 3 tablespoons olive oil

- 2 cloves garlic, minced
- 1 tomato, chopped
- 1 tablespoon lemon juice
- salt and pepper to taste

DIRECTIONS

1. In a large bowl, combine the chickpeas, red onion, garlic, tomato, parsley, olive oil, lemon juice and salt and pepper to taste. Chill for 2 hours before serving. Taste and adjust seasoning. Serve.

APRICOT LENTIL SOUP
Servings: 6 | Prep: 15m | Cooks: 50m | Total: 1h5m

NUTRITION FACTS

Calories: 263.2 | Carbohydrates: 37.2g | Protein: 13.2g | Cholesterol: 0mg | Sodium: 6.6mg

INGREDIENTS

- 3 tablespoons olive oil
- 3 roma (plum) tomatoes - peeled, seeded and chopped

- 1 onion, chopped
- 2 cloves garlic, minced
- 1/3 cup dried apricots
- 1 1/2 cups red lentils
- 5 cups chicken stock
- 1/2 teaspoon ground cumin
- 1/2 teaspoon dried thyme
- salt to taste
- ground black pepper to taste
- 2 tablespoons fresh lemon juice

DIRECTIONS

1. Saute onion, garlic, and apricots in olive oil. Add lentils and stock. Bring to a boil, then reduce heat and simmer 30 minutes.
2. Stir in tomatoes, and season with cumin, thyme, and salt and pepper to taste. Simmer for 10 minutes.
3. Stir in lemon juice. Puree 1/2 of the soup in a blender, then return to the pot. Serve.

MUSHROOM LENTIL BARLEY STEW
Servings: 8 | Prep: 15m | Cooks: 12h | Total: 12h15m

NUTRITION FACTS

Calories: 213 | Carbohydrates: 43.9g | Fat: 1.2g | Protein: 8.4g | Cholesterol: 0mg | Sodium: 466mg

INGREDIENTS

- 2 quarts vegetable broth
- 2 cups sliced fresh button mushrooms
- 1 ounce dried shiitake mushrooms, torn into pieces
- 3/4 cup uncooked pearl barley
- 3/4 cup dry lentils
- 1/4 cup dried onion flakes
- 2 teaspoons minced garlic
- 2 teaspoons dried summer savory
- 3 bay leaves
- 1 teaspoon dried basil
- 2 teaspoons ground black pepper
- salt to taste

DIRECTIONS

1. In a slow cooker, mix the broth, button mushrooms, shiitake mushrooms, barley, lentils, onion flakes, garlic, savory, bay leaves, basil, pepper, and salt.
2. Cover, and cook 4 to 6 hours on High or 10 to 12 hours on Low. Remove bay leaves before serving.

QUICK AND EASY REFRIED BEANS

Servings: 6 | Prep: 10m | Cooks: 10m | Total: 20m

NUTRITION FACTS

Calories: 131.7 | Carbohydrates: 16.1g | Protein: 5g | Cholesterol: 0mg | Sodium: 323.2mg

INGREDIENTS

- 2 tablespoons canola oil
- 2 garlic clove (blank)s garlic cloves, peeled
- 2 (15 ounce) cans pinto beans
- 1 teaspoon cumin
- 1 teaspoon chili powder
- 1 pinch salt to taste
- 1/2 lime, juiced

DIRECTIONS

1. Heat canola oil in a heavy skillet over medium heat.
2. Cook garlic cloves in hot oil, turning once, until brown on both sides, 4 to 5 minutes.
3. Smash garlic cloves in skillet with a fork.
4. Stir pinto beans, cumin, chili powder, and salt into mashed garlic and cook until beans are thoroughly heated, about 5 minutes. Stir occasionally.
5. Smash bean mixture with a potato masher to desired texture. Squeeze lime juice over smashed beans and stir until combined.

CHILI CON CARNE
Servings: 10 | Prep: 20m | Cooks: 45m | Total: 1h5m

NUTRITION FACTS

Calories: 397 | Carbohydrates: 32.5g | Protein: 23.9g | Cholesterol: 61.5mg | Sodium: 916.8mg

INGREDIENTS

- 5 tablespoons vegetable oil

- 2 large onions, chopped

- 1 chile pepper, chopped

- 5 cloves garlic, chopped

- 2 pounds lean ground beef

- 3 (14.5 ounce) cans whole peeled tomatoes with liquid, chopped

- 1 1/2 teaspoons salt

- 1 1/2 tablespoons ground cumin

- 1/2 tablespoon chili powder

- 2 tablespoons paprika

- 2 tablespoons dried oregano

- 2 cinnamon sticks

- 6 eaches whole cloves

- 2 (15.25 ounce) cans red kidney beans, rinsed and drained

- 1 teaspoon freshly ground black pepper

DIRECTIONS

1. In a medium sized stock pot, heat the oil over medium heat. Saute onion, chile pepper and garlic until soft. Add ground beef: cook and stir until meat is browned.
2. Pour in tomatoes with liquid, salt, pepper, cumin, chili powder, paprika, oregano, cinnamon sticks, and cloves. Cover and simmer for 45 minutes.
3. Stir in kidney beans, and cook another 15 minutes. Remove cinnamon sticks before serving.

SLOW COOKER LENTILS AND SAUSAGE

Servings: 12 | Prep: 15m | Cooks: 3h | Total: 3h15m

NUTRITION FACTS

Calories: 357.3 | Carbohydrates: 22.8g | Protein: 18.8g | Cholesterol: 49.9mg | Sodium: 966.3mg

INGREDIENTS

- 1 (16 ounce) package dry lentils
- 1 carrot, chopped

- 1 (16 ounce) can diced tomatoes, drained
- 2 pounds kielbasa (Polish) sausage, cut into 1/2 inch pieces
- 2 (14 ounce) cans beef broth
- 1 stalk celery, chopped
- 3 cups water

DIRECTIONS

1. Rinse and drain lentils, but do not soak. In a slow cooker, stir together the lentils, tomatoes, broth, water, carrot, sausage, and celery.
2. Cover, and cook on High for 3 hours, or Low for 6 to 7 hours. Stir well before serving.

MICHELLE'S BLONDE CHICKEN CHILI

Servings: 10 | Prep: 30m | Cooks: 30m | Total: 1h

NUTRITION FACTS

Calories: 411.9 | Carbohydrates: 46.6g | Protein: 47.2g | Cholesterol: 79.1mg | Sodium: 361.6mg

INGREDIENTS

- 1 tablespoon vegetable oil
- 1 tablespoon garlic powder

- 3 pounds skinless, boneless chicken breast meat - cubed

- 1 cup chopped onion

- 2 cups chicken broth

- 2 (4 ounce) cans chopped green chile peppers

- 5 (14.5 ounce) cans great Northern beans, undrained

- 1 tablespoon ground cumin

- 1 tablespoon dried oregano

- 2 teaspoons chopped fresh cilantro

- 1 teaspoon crushed red pepper

DIRECTIONS

1. In a large skillet over medium-high heat, place the vegetable oil and chicken. Cook the chicken, stirring occasionally, until all pieces are evenly brown. Stir in the onions. Cook until translucent. Drain mixture and set aside.
2. In a large saucepan over medium heat, bring the chicken broth and green chile peppers to a boil. Stir in 3 cans great northern beans, garlic powder, cumin, oregano, cilantro and

crushed red pepper. Stir in the chicken and onion mixture, and reduce heat. Simmer 30 minutes or longer, adding additional beans from the remaining cans for a thicker consistency as desired.

QUICK BLACK BEANS AND RICE

Servings: 4 | Prep: 5m | Cooks: 15m | Total: 25m | Additional: 5m

NUTRITION FACTS

Calories: 271.4 | Carbohydrates: 47.8g | Protein: 10g | Cholesterol: 0mg | Sodium: 552.4mg

INGREDIENTS

- 1 tablespoon vegetable oil
- 1 onion, chopped
- 1 (15 ounce) can black beans, undrained
- 1 (14.5 ounce) can stewed tomatoes
- 1 teaspoon dried oregano
- 1/2 teaspoon garlic powder
- 1 1/2 cups uncooked instant brown rice

DIRECTIONS

1. In large saucepan, heat oil over medium-high. Add onion, cook and stir until tender. Add beans, tomatoes, oregano and garlic powder. Bring to a boil; stir in rice. Cover; reduce

heat and simmer 5 minutes. Remove from heat; let stand 5 minutes before serving.

JALAPENO HUMMUS

Servings: 8 | Prep: 10m | Cooks: 0m | Total: 10m

NUTRITION FACTS

Calories: 74.6 | Carbohydrates: 9.1g | Protein: 2.6g | Cholesterol: 0mg | Sodium: 191.4mg

INGREDIENTS

- 1 cup garbanzo beans
- 1/3 cup canned jalapeno pepper slices, juice reserved
- 3 tablespoons tahini
- 3 cloves garlic, minced
- 2 tablespoons lemon juice
- 1/2 teaspoon ground cumin
- 1/2 teaspoon curry powder
- 1 pinch crushed red pepper to taste

DIRECTIONS

1. In a blender or food processor, mix the garbanzo beans, jalapeno peppers and reserved juice, tahini, garlic, and lemon juice. Season with cumin, curry powder, and crushed red pepper. Blend until smooth.

VEGETARIAN CHILI
Servings: 6 | Prep: 10m | Cooks: 1h | Total: 1h10m

NUTRITION FACTS

Calories: 582.1 | Carbohydrates: 74.2g | Protein: 67.5g | Cholesterol: 0mg | Sodium: 2000.1mg

INGREDIENTS

- 1 (12 ounce) package frozen burger-style crumbles
- 2 (15 ounce) cans black beans, rinsed and drained
- 2 (15 ounce) cans dark red kidney beans
- 5 onions, chopped
- 3 tablespoons chili powder
- 1 1/2 tablespoons ground cumin

- 1 (15 ounce) can light red kidney beans
- 1 (29 ounce) can diced tomatoes
- 1 (12 fluid ounce) can tomato juice
- 1 tablespoon garlic powder
- 2 eaches bay leaves
- salt and pepper to taste

DIRECTIONS

1. In a large pot, combine meat substitute, black beans, kidney beans, diced tomatoes, tomato juice, onions, chili powder, cumin, garlic powder, bay leaves, salt and pepper. Bring to a simmer and cover. Let the chili simmer for at least 1 hour before serving.

APPLE BACON TOMATO SOUP

Servings: 8 | Prep: 15m | Cooks: 30m | Total: 45m

NUTRITION FACTS

Calories: 194.6 | Carbohydrates: 16.6g | Protein: 6.4g | Cholesterol: 11.9mg | Sodium: 446.8mg

INGREDIENTS

- 5 slices bacon
- 1 tablespoon olive oil
- 1/2 white onion, chopped
- 2 teaspoons garlic, minced
- 2 cups beef stock
- 1 (15.5 ounce) can pinto beans
- 1 (14.5 ounce) can Italian-style stewed tomatoes
- 2 stalks celery, chopped
- 1 bay leaf
- 1 medium apple, thinly sliced
- 1/2 cup red wine
- salt and pepper to taste

DIRECTIONS

1. Place bacon in a large, deep skillet. Cook over medium high heat until evenly brown. Drain, coarsely chop, and set aside.

2. Heat olive oil in a large saucepan over medium heat, and saute white onion and garlic 3 to 5 minutes, or until tender. Stir in beef stock, pinto beans, tomatoes, celery, and bay leaf. Bring the mixture to a boil. Reduce heat, and simmer.
3. In a small saucepan over medium heat, cook and stir the apple in the red wine until soft.
4. Mix bacon, apple, and remaining red wine into the soup mixture. Season with salt and pepper. Continue to simmer, stirring occasionally until well blended.

LENTIL SOUP

Servings: 8 | Prep: 5m | Cooks: 30m | Total: 35m

NUTRITION FACTS

Calories: 155.9 | Carbohydrates: 27.7g | Protein: 11.5g | Cholesterol: 0mg | Sodium: 68.9mg

INGREDIENTS

- 2 cups dry lentils
- 2 quarts chicken broth
- 1 onion, diced
- 1/4 cup tomato paste
- 2 cloves garlic, minced
- 1 tablespoon ground cumin

DIRECTIONS

1. In a large saucepan combine lentils, broth, onion, tomato paste, garlic and cumin. Bring to a boil, then reduce heat, cover and simmer until lentils are soft, 30 to 45 minutes. Serve with a squeeze of lemon.

TOMATO-CURRY LENTIL STEW
Servings: 2 | Prep: 10m | Cooks: 50m | Total: 1h

NUTRITION FACTS

Calories: 205.6 | Carbohydrates: 36.9g | Protein: 13.7g | Cholesterol: 0mg | Sodium: 194.4mg

INGREDIENTS

- 1/2 cup dry lentils
- 1 cup water
- 5 ounces stewed tomatoes
- 1/8 cup chopped onion
- 1/4 teaspoon curry powder
- 3 cloves garlic, minced
- salt to taste
- ground black pepper to taste

- 2 stalks celery, chopped, with leaves

DIRECTIONS

1. Combine lentils and water, bring to a boil.
2. Lower heat to simmer, add tomatoes, onion, and celery. Cover and let simmer 45 minutes. Check every 15 minutes to stir, and add water if necessary. Add spices last 15 minutes to taste. Taste and re-spice if necessary before serving.

TASTY LENTIL TACOS

Servings: 6 | Prep: 10m | Cooks: 40m | Total: 50m

NUTRITION FACTS

Calories: 304 | Carbohydrates: 44.2g | Fat: 10g | Protein: 9.4g | Cholesterol: 1mg | Sodium: 714mg

INGREDIENTS

- 1 teaspoon canola oil
- 1 tablespoon taco seasoning, or to taste
- 2/3 cup finely chopped onion
- 1 2/3 cups chicken broth
- 1 small clove garlic, minced
- 2/3 cup salsa

- 2/3 cup dried lentils, rinsed
- 12 taco shells

DIRECTIONS

1. Heat oil in a skillet over medium heat; cook and stir onion and garlic until tender, about 5 minutes. Mix lentils and taco seasoning into onion mixture; cook and stir for 1 minute.
2. Pour chicken broth into skillet and bring to a boil. Reduce heat to low, cover the skillet, and simmer until lentils are tender, 25 to 30 minutes.
3. Uncover the skillet and cook until mixture is slightly thickened, 6 to 8 minutes. Mash lentils slightly; stir in salsa.
4. Serve about 1/4 cup lentil mixture in each taco shell.

CHICKEN AND LENTILS

Servings: 6 | Prep: 15m | Cooks: 1h15m | Total: 1h30m

NUTRITION FACTS

Calories: 308.3 | Carbohydrates: 18.7g | Protein: 27.8g | Cholesterol: 68.1mg | Sodium: 816.5mg

INGREDIENTS

- 1 tablespoon olive oil
- 1 (14 ounce) can chicken broth

- 2 pounds bone-in chicken pieces
- 1 large onion, finely chopped
- 1 small carrot, finely chopped
- 2 cloves garlic, finely chopped
- 3/4 cup dried lentils
- 1/2 teaspoon salt
- 1 (10 ounce) can tomato sauce
- 1/2 teaspoon dried rosemary
- 1/2 teaspoon dried basil
- 1 tablespoon lemon juice

DIRECTIONS

1. Heat the oil in a skillet over medium heat, and cook the chicken pieces 5 minutes on each side, or until juices run clear. Remove chicken from skillet, and set aside.
2. Place onion in the skillet, and cook 5 minutes, until tender. Mix in the carrot and garlic. Stir in the lentils and broth, and season with salt. Bring to a boil, cover, reduce heat to low, and simmer 20 minutes.
3. Return chicken to skillet. Cover, and continue cooking 20 minutes. If the mixture becomes too dry, add a little water to just moisten.

4. Stir tomato sauce into the skillet. Season with rosemary and basil. Continue cooking 10 minutes, or until lentils are tender. Stir in lemon juice, and serve warm.

COWBOY CAVIAR

Servings: 8 | Prep: 20m | Cooks: 20m | Total: 40m | Additional: 20m

NUTRITION FACTS

Calories: 233.4 | Carbohydrates: 32.3g | Protein: 7.9g | Cholesterol: 0mg | Sodium: 1255.3mg

INGREDIENTS

- 1 (15.5 ounce) can black beans, drained
- 1 (15.5 ounce) can black-eyed peas, drained
- 1 (14.5 ounce) can diced tomatoes, drained
- 2 cups frozen corn kernels, thawed
- 1/4 green bell pepper, finely chopped
- 1/2 cup chopped pickled jalapeno peppers
- 1/2 teaspoon garlic salt
- 1 cup Italian salad dressing

- 1/2 medium onion, chopped
- 3/4 cup chopped cilantro

DIRECTIONS

1. Mix beans, peas, tomatoes, corn, onion, bell pepper, and jalapeno peppers in a large bowl. Season with garlic salt. Add dressing and cilantro; toss to coat. Refrigerate for 20 minutes or until ready to serve.

TACO SALAD

Servings: 8 | Prep: 15m | Cooks: 15m | Total: 30m

NUTRITION FACTS

Calories: 945.3 | Carbohydrates: 75.7g | Protein: 27.3g | Cholesterol: 72.3mg | Sodium: 1682mg

INGREDIENTS

- 16 ounces lean ground beef
- 1 (1.25 ounce) package taco seasoning mix
- 1 head iceberg lettuce, shredded
- 1 red onion, sliced
- 1 bunch green onions, chopped
- 1 (15 ounce) can pinto beans, drained
- 1 (15 ounce) can kidney beans, drained
- 2 large tomatoes, chopped
- 1 avocados - peeled, pitted, and cubed
- 8 ounces shredded Cheddar cheese
- 1 (16 ounce) package corn chips
- 1 (16 ounce) bottle Catalina salad dressing

DIRECTIONS

1. Prepare the ground beef as directed by taco seasoning package and set aside.

2. In a large bowl, combine the beef mixture, lettuce, red onion, green onion, pinto beans, kidney beans, tomatoes, avocado and cheese. Mix well.
3. Before serving, add the corn chips and enough dressing to coat. Mix well and serve immediately.

MEXICAN BEAN AND RICE SALAD
Servings: 10 | Prep: 20m | Cooks: 0m | Total: 1h20m

NUTRITION FACTS

Calories: 162 | Carbohydrates: 33g | Fat: 1.1g | Protein: 7.2g | Cholesterol: 0mg | Sodium: 399mg

INGREDIENTS

- 2 cups cooked brown rice
- 1 (15 ounce) can kidney beans, rinsed and drained
- 1 (15 ounce) can black beans, rinsed and drained
- 1 (15.25 ounce) can whole kernel corn,
- 2 jalapeno peppers, seeded and diced
- 1 lime, zested and juiced
- 1/4 cup chopped cilantro leaves
- 1 teaspoon minced garlic

- drained

- 1 small onion, diced
- 1 1/2 teaspoons ground cumin

- 1 green bell pepper, diced
- salt to taste

DIRECTIONS

1. In a large salad bowl, combine the brown rice, kidney beans, black beans, corn, onion, green pepper, jalapeno peppers, lime zest and juice, cilantro, garlic, and cumin. Lightly toss all ingredients to mix well, and sprinkle with salt to taste.
2. Refrigerate salad for 1 hour, toss again, and serve.

SMOKY CHIPOTLE HUMMUS

Servings: 20 | Prep: 15m | Cooks: 0m | Total: 15m

NUTRITION FACTS

Calories: 89.6 | Carbohydrates: 11.9g | Protein: 2.9g | Cholesterol: 0mg | Sodium: 235.3mg

INGREDIENTS

- 2 (15.5 ounce) cans garbanzo beans,
- 1 1/2 teaspoons cumin

drained

- 1/2 cup water

- 1/4 cup tahini (sesame-seed paste)

- 1/4 cup fresh lemon juice

- 2 tablespoons olive oil

- 1 canned chipotle pepper in adobo sauce

- 2 cloves garlic

- 1 (7 ounce) jar roasted red bell peppers, drained

- 6 oil-packed sun-dried tomatoes, drained

- 1/2 cup chopped cilantro

- 1/2 teaspoon salt

- 1 pinch ground black pepper to taste

DIRECTIONS

1. Place the garbanzo beans, water, tahini, lemon juice, olive oil, chipotle pepper, garlic, and cumin in the bowl of a food processor; blend until smooth. Add the red peppers, sun-dried tomatoes, cilantro, salt, and pepper. Pulse the mixture until the ingredients are coarsely chopped into the hummus

base. Transfer to a serving bowl, cover, and chill until ready to serve.

SOUTHERN HAM AND BROWN BEANS

Servings: 8 | Prep: 10m | Cooks: 3h | Total: 3h10m

NUTRITION FACTS

Calories: 272.5 | Carbohydrates: 37.7g | Protein: 16.7g | Cholesterol: 17mg | Sodium: 322.6mg

INGREDIENTS

- 1 pound dry pinto beans
- 8 cups water
- 1 large, meaty ham hock
- 1 large onion, chopped
- 2 cloves garlic, minced
- 1 teaspoon chili powder
- 1 teaspoon salt, or to taste
- 1/4 teaspoon ground black pepper, or to taste

DIRECTIONS

1. Place the beans and water in a large stockpot. Add the ham hock, onion and garlic. Season with chili powder, salt and pepper. Bring to a boil, and cook for 2 minutes. Cover, and remove from heat. Let stand for one hour.
2. Return the pot to the heat, and bring to a boil once again. Reduce heat to medium-low, and simmer for at least 3 hours to blend flavors. The longer you simmer, the thicker the broth will become. I like to cook mine for about 6 hours.
3. Remove the ham hock from the broth, and let cool. Remove the meat from the bone, and return the meat to the stockpot, discarding the bone. Adjust seasonings to taste.

PUB-STYLE VEGETARIAN CHILI
Servings: 8 | Prep: 30m | Cooks: 25m | Total: 55m

NUTRITION FACTS

Calories: 223.6 | Carbohydrates: 27.2g | Protein: 8.1g | Cholesterol: 0mg | Sodium: 929.5mg

INGREDIENTS

- 1/3 cup olive oil
- 2 cups sliced fresh mushrooms
- 3/4 teaspoon ground black pepper
- 3/4 teaspoon dried basil

- 1 cup finely chopped onion
- 1 cup chopped carrot
- 3/4 cup chopped green bell pepper
- 1/4 cup chopped celery
- 1 tablespoon minced garlic
- 1 tablespoon chili powder, or more to taste
- 1 tablespoon ground cumin
- 1 1/8 teaspoons salt
- 3/4 teaspoon dried oregano
- 1 (28 ounce) can whole peeled tomatoes with juice
- 3 cups black beans, undrained
- 1/2 (6 ounce) can tomato paste
- 1/4 cup red wine
- 3/4 teaspoon hot pepper sauce (such as Tabasco®)
- 2 cups water

DIRECTIONS

1. Heat olive oil in a large pot over medium heat; cook and stir mushrooms, onion, carrot, green bell pepper, celery, garlic, chili powder, cumin, salt, black pepper, basil, and oregano until the onion begins to soften, 2 to 3 minutes.
2. Stir in tomatoes with their liquid, black beans and their liquid, tomato paste, red wine, hot pepper sauce, and water.
3. Bring the chili to a boil, reduce heat to low, and simmer until vegetables are tender, about 20 minutes.

VEGETARIAN TORTILLA STEW

Servings: 4 | Prep: 15m | Cooks: 15m | Total: 30m

NUTRITION FACTS

Calories: 347 | Carbohydrates: 42.5g | Protein: 16.4g | Cholesterol: 24.7mg | Sodium: 565.3mg

INGREDIENTS

- 1 (19 ounce) can green enchilada sauce
- 1 1/2 cups water
- 1 cube vegetable bouillon
- 1/2 (16 ounce) can diced tomatoes
- 1 cup frozen corn
- 1/2 cup vegetarian chicken substitute, diced

- 1/2 teaspoon garlic powder
- 1/4 teaspoon chili powder
- 1/4 teaspoon ground cumin
- 1 (15 ounce) can pinto beans, drained and rinsed
- 4 (6 inch) corn tortillas, torn into strips
- 1 tablespoon chopped fresh cilantro
- 1 pinch salt and pepper to taste

DIRECTIONS

1. In a pot, mix the enchilada sauce and water. Dissolve the bouillon cube in the liquid, and season with garlic powder, chile powder, and cumin. Bring to a boil, and reduce heat to low. Mix in the beans, tomatoes, and corn. Simmer until heated through. Mix in vegetarian chicken and tortillas, and cook until heated through. Stir in cilantro, and season with salt and pepper to serve.

VEGETARIAN TORTILLA STEW

Servings: 6 | Prep: 25m | Cooks: 25m | Total: 32m

NUTRITION FACTS

Calories: 317.4 | Carbohydrates: 35.2g | Protein: 7.2g | Cholesterol: 0mg | Sodium: 723.9mg

INGREDIENTS

- 1 (19 ounce) can garbanzo beans, rinsed and drained
- 1 small onion, finely chopped
- 2 cloves garlic, minced
- 1 1/2 tablespoons chopped fresh cilantro
- 1 teaspoon dried parsley
- 2 teaspoons ground cumin
- 1/8 teaspoon ground turmeric
- 1/2 teaspoon baking powder
- 1 cup fine dry bread crumbs
- 3/4 teaspoon salt
- 1/4 teaspoon cracked black peppercorns
- 1 quart vegetable oil for frying

DIRECTIONS

1. Mash the garbanzo beans in a large bowl. Stir in the onion, garlic, cilantro, parsley, cumin, turmeric, baking powder, bread crumbs, salt and pepper. Do not be afraid to use your hands. Shape the mixture into 1 1/2 inch balls; you should get 18 to 24. If the mixture does not hold together, add a little water.
2. eat the oil in a deep fryer to 375 degrees F (190 degrees C). Carefully drop the balls into the hot oil, and fry until brown. If you do not have a deep fryer, heat the oil in a heavy deep skillet over medium-high heat. You may need to adjust the heat slightly after the first couple of falafels, and be sure to turn frequently so they brown evenly.

INDIAN DAHL WITH SPINACH
Servings: 4 | Prep: 10m | Cooks: 30m | Total: 40m
NUTRITION FACTS

Calories: 362 | Carbohydrates: 44.9g | Protein: 21g | Cholesterol: 15.3mg | Sodium: 692.6mg

INGREDIENTS

- 1 1/2 cups red lentils
- 3 1/2 cups water
- 1/2 teaspoon salt
- 2 tablespoons butter
- 1 onion, chopped
- 1 teaspoon ground cumin

- 1/2 teaspoon ground turmeric
- 1/2 teaspoon chili powder
- 1 pound spinach, rinsed and chopped
- 1 teaspoon mustard seed
- 1 teaspoon garam masala
- 1/2 cup coconut milk

DIRECTIONS

1. Rinse lentils and soak for 20 minutes.
2. In a large saucepan, bring water to a boil and stir in salt, lentils, turmeric and chili powder. Cover and return to a boil, then reduce heat to low and simmer for 15 minutes. Stir in the spinach and cook 5 minutes, or until lentils are soft. Add more water if necessary.
3. In a small saucepan over medium heat, melt butter and saute onions with cumin and mustard seeds, stirring often. Cook until onions are transparent, and then combine with lentils. Stir in garam masala and coconut milk and cook until heated through.

BEST BEAN SALAD
Servings: 18 | Prep: 20m | Cooks: 0m | Total: 8h20m | Additional: 8h

NUTRITION FACTS

Calories: 167.3 | Carbohydrates: 23.6g | Protein: 4.4g | Cholesterol: 0mg | Sodium: 412.1mg

INGREDIENTS

- 1 (14.5 ounce) can green beans, drained
- 1 (14.5 ounce) can wax beans, drained
- 1 (15.5 ounce) can garbanzo beans, drained
- 1 (14.5 ounce) can kidney beans, drained
- 1 (14.5 ounce) can black beans, drained
- 1/2 cup chopped green pepper
- 1/2 cup chopped onion
- 1/2 cup chopped celery
- 1/2 cup salad oil
- 1/2 cup vinegar
- 1/2 teaspoon salt
- 1/2 teaspoon ground black pepper
- 3/4 cup white sugar

DIRECTIONS

1. Combine the green beans, wax beans, garbanzo beans, kidney beans, green pepper, onion, and celery in a large bowl; toss to mix.
2. Whisk together the oil, vinegar, salt, pepper, and sugar in a separate bowl until the sugar is dissolved; pour over the bean mixture. Refrigerate 8 hours or overnight before serving.

BAKED FALAFEL

Servings: 2 | Prep: 20m | Cooks: 20m | Total: 55m | Additional: 15m

NUTRITION FACTS

Calories: 167.3 | Carbohydrates: 23.6g | Protein: 4.4g | Cholesterol: 0mg | Sodium: 412.1mg

INGREDIENTS

- 1/4 cup chopped onion
- 1 (15 ounce) can garbanzo beans, rinsed and drained
- 1/4 cup chopped fresh parsley
- 3 cloves garlic, minced
- 1/4 teaspoon salt
- 1/4 teaspoon baking soda
- 1 tablespoon all-purpose flour
- 1 egg, beaten

- 1 teaspoon ground cumin

- 2 teaspoons olive oil

- 1/4 teaspoon ground coriander

DIRECTIONS

1. Wrap onion in cheese cloth and squeeze out as much moisture as possible. Set aside. Place garbanzo beans, parsley, garlic, cumin, coriander, salt, and baking soda in a food processor. Process until the mixture is coarsely pureed. Mix garbanzo bean mixture and onion together in a bowl. Stir in the flour and egg. Shape mixture into four large patties and let stand for 15 minutes.
2. Preheat an oven to 400 degrees F (200 degrees C).
3. Heat olive oil in a large, oven-safe skillet over medium-high heat. Place the patties in the skillet; cook until golden brown, about 3 minutes on each side.
4. Transfer skillet to the preheated oven and bake until heated through, about 10 minutes.

ENCHILADA CASSEROLE

Servings: 8 | Prep: 15m | Cooks: 45m | Total: 1h

NUTRITION FACTS

Calories: 375.2 | Carbohydrates: 24.9g | Protein: 17.4g | Cholesterol: 54mg | Sodium: 709.2mg

INGREDIENTS

- 1 (15 ounce) can black beans, rinsed and drained
- 2 cloves garlic, minced
- 1 onion, chopped
- 1 (4 ounce) can diced green chile peppers
- 1 jalapeno pepper, seeded and minced
- 1 (8 ounce) package tempeh, crumbled
- 6 (6 inch) corn tortillas
- 1 (19 ounce) can enchilada sauce
- 1 (6 ounce) can sliced black olives
- 8 ounces shredded Cheddar cheese

DIRECTIONS

1. Preheat oven to 350 degrees (175 degrees C). Lightly oil a 9x13 inch baking dish.
2. In a medium bowl, combine the beans, garlic, onion, chile peppers, jalapeno pepper, and tempeh. Pour enchilada sauce into a shallow bowl.
3. Dip three tortillas in the enchilada sauce, and place them in the prepared baking dish. Be sure to cover the bottom of the dish as completely as possible. Place 1/2 of the bean mixture on top of the tortillas, and repeat. Drizzle the

remaining sauce over the casserole, and sprinkle with olives and shredded cheese.
4. Cover, and bake for 30 minutes. Uncover, and continue baking for an additional 15 minutes, or until the casserole is bubbling and the cheese is melted.

Printed in Great Britain
by Amazon